Liberating the Nations

Liberating the Nations

Biblical Principles of Government, Education, Economics, & Politics

Stephen McDowell &
Mark Beliles

Providence Foundation

Charlottesville, Virginia

Liberating the Nations:
Biblical Principles of Government, Education, Economics, & Politics

First Printing, 1991
Second Printing, 1993
Third Printing, 1995

Published by:
The Providence Foundation
P.O. Box 6759
Charlottesville, VA 22906
(804) 978-4535

Cover design:
Jeremiah Pent
Graphicom
P.O. Box 10720
Ft. Worth, TX 76114
(817) 625-5500

*The Providence Foundation is a Christian educational organization
whose purpose is to assist in the development of liberty, justice, and
prosperity among the nations by teaching and equipping people in a
Biblical philosophy of life. The Foundation teaches Christian principles of government and politics, economics and business, arts and
sciences, education and family life, using historical models which illustrate their application.*

Printed in the United States of America

ISBN 1-887456-01-5

Liberating the Nations

Table of Contents

Introduction

We have entitled this book, *Liberating the Nations, Biblical Principles of Government, Education, Economics, & Politics*. This title will evoke many questions, such as: Can nations in a fallen, sinful world be liberated? If so, how can liberty come to nations? Does the Bible contain principles that apply to public life? If so, can these biblical principles produce godly change in nations that apply them?

We had considered entitling this book, *Fundamentals for Building Christian Nations*, which accurately describes the goal of this work. Such a title would also raise many questions, the chief one being: "Is there such a thing as a Christian nation?" If so, what is a Christian nation and how is one built? These questions and much more are answered in this book.

There are most certainly nations where the Christian religion is embraced as the majority faith, as there are also muslim nations and hindu nations. In fact, every nation is built upon some religion or philosophy of life. (This includes the "religion" of humanism, which is where man is god, and he is the final source of what is right and wrong, which is reflected in the law of a society.) However, a Christian nation, as we use the term, is not one that simply has a majority Christian populace, nor is it a nation that is run by the church or some ecclesiastical body. Europe in the Middle Ages had many Catholic nations where this was the case. Rather, a Christian nation is one that is founded upon Christian principles, whose laws and institutions reflect a Christian world-view. The Bible teaches, and history confirms, that to the degree that nations have applied the principles of the Bible in all spheres of life, is the degree to which they have prospered, been free, and acted justly.

"Where the Spirit of the Lord is, there is liberty." This is true for men and nations. As the gospel goes into a man's heart, he is changed. Likewise, as the gospel is infused in the life of nation, it is changed.

God changes nations from the internal to the external. Therefore, to liberate a nation, we must first liberate the people of a nation. This will occur as we preach the gospel, as Jesus commanded, and then teach believers how to live out the truth of the Bible in their everyday life. 2 Chronicles 7:14 reveals to us the importance of repentance and prayer for the transforming of nations. This is obviously where all godly change must begin. Since much has been written and taught on these topics, we have not dealt with them in great detail in this book, although we understand no permanent positive change will occur without a heart change first occurring in the citizens of a nation.

This book is to supplement all the good material that is available that addresses personal evangelism and prayer in changing men and nations. After God changes the hearts of men, what then? When men are changed, their families, businesses, schools, churches, neighborhoods, towns, cities, states, and nations should also change. The principles of the Bible affect all of life, including families, education, churches, the media, government, economics, and business. In *Liberating the Nations* we attempt to provide principles from the Bible that apply to these areas. Our goal is by no means to be exhaustive, but merely introduce in a general way to the citizens of nations a framework for building their societies in accordance with a Biblical view of life.

Those who are familiar with our book, *America's Providential History*, will recognize some similarities between it and *Liberating the Nations*. This is especially true of the chapters on economics, education, the church, and the chain of liberty. The reason for this is that what we wished to accomplish in America with *America's Providential History*, is similar to what we wish to accomplish in all nations with *Liberating the Nations*. Both books are designed to teach a biblical world-view, equip Christians in principles of self- and civil government, and inspire action. However, there is a great deal of research in this book that was not in *America's Providential History*, and there is, of course, less American history. Our desire is for individuals to not only read the book, but for it to also be used as a textbook in classes and discussion groups that people start in their churches, schools, and organizations. Thousands of people in scores of countries have already been using an earlier edition of this book. Many changes have been made with this edition, and many more will probably need to be made in future editions. As we continue to learn how God's principles of liberty apply to nations and how best to communicate these principles to the general populace, we will continue to revise this work. We invite the reader to give us constructive input to help make it a better, more understandable and relevant book in the future. We also welcome any requests to translate it and add local statistics and historical information for indigenous printings.

This book represents our attempt, in a small way, to equip people to "go... and make disciples of all the nations," by "teaching them to observe all that [He] commanded" (Matthew 28:19). It is given with the prayer that the kingdoms of this world will become, in their actions and acknowledgements, the kingdoms of our Lord and of His Christ.

Section 1

God's Principles and Plan for Liberating the Nations

Chapter 1

The Fundamental Principles of Christian Nations

The world is changing rapidly today. Nations are crying out for freedom and are looking for ways to bring prosperity to their lands. While we have witnessed the fall of communism, and see the possibility for continued positive change to take place in the world, the potential for national upheavals is also great.

Most nations are facing tremendous problems. Individuals, families, businesses, and nations are crumbling or on the verge of crumbling. Pressures are mounting on every aspect of society today.

How are we to hold up under such pressures? Where are we to look for answers to the many problems and difficult situations we face? The Bible provides the answers the world seeks. The truth contained in the Bible provides mankind with principles of liberty that brings real freedom to those individuals and nations who are oppressed (John 8:32).

The Bible teaches and history confirms that to the degree that a nation applies the principles of the Word of God to all aspects of the society is the degree to which that nation obtains freedom and prosperity.

The principles contained in the Bible encompass all of life. This includes divine matters between man and God, but also social and civil matters. Just as the Truth will set men free as they act upon it, so shall it also set nations free that abide by it.

Jesus instructed His disciples to take the Gospel message to all the nations. While much of the church in recent generations has limited the message of the gospel to personal matters, the Bible reveals the Gospel message encom-

3

passes all of life. We can summarize the areas the Gospel affects with the following:

1. Personal conversion

2. Divine institutions

  a. Family
  b. Church
  d. Civil Government

3. Spiritual warfare

As the church goes to fulfill the great commission it must affect every one of these areas. These include the major components of society -- the individual, family, church, volunteer associations, and civil government.

A Nation's Foundation Must Be Strong to Hold Up Under Pressure

For a nation or society to stand under pressure it must have a strong foundation. This means that each component of society must have a strong foundation. Francis Schaeffer stated that an individual, family, church, association, or government *"with a weak base can stand only when the pressure on it is not too great."* He gave the illustration of relating a person and culture to a Roman bridge:

"The Romans built little humpbacked bridges over many of the streams of Europe. People and wagons went over these structures safely for centuries, for two millennia. But if people today drove heavily loaded trucks over these bridges, they would break. It is this way with lives and value systems of individuals and cultures when they have nothing stronger to build on than their own limitedness, their own finiteness. They can stand when pressures are not too great, but when pressures mount, if then they do not have a sufficient base, they crash -- just as a Roman bridge would cave in under the weight of a modern six-wheeled truck. Culture and the freedoms of people are fragile. Without a sufficient base, when such pressures come only time is needed -- and often not a great deal of time -- before there is a collapse." [1]

The pressures that people and nations face today are so great that they will quickly collapse unless they are supported with a solid foundation. That foundation is composed of principles found in the Bible. Figure 1 illustrates the components of society as layers of a bridge, with the foundations

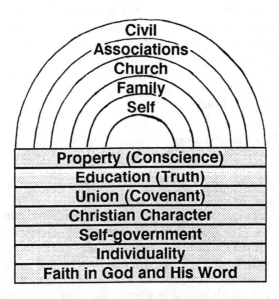

Figure 1. The Fundamental Principles that Support Christian Nations

necessary to support a free, just, prosperous, and long-lasting nation.

As we work to bring reformation to the nations, we must remember that change begins internally. Nations seeking to shift from communistic economic systems to a free market (or from state control to more self-government) must recognize that they will never accomplish their goals unless the people have the proper foundation in character and thought.

It is not enough to set up external structures, even if they have worked in other nations and have been part of the best and most free governments in history. We must remember that good structures are not enough because the best government in ill hands can do nothing great or good.

The following foundations in individuals, families, churches, associations, and governments will provide a strong base allowing each component of society, and hence society itself, to stand up under any pressure. These principles must be part of the lives of the people of any nation desiring freedom and prosperity, for after all, it is men who cause governments to run. Governments depend upon men more than men depend upon governments. If men are good, the government cannot be bad.

These principles form the basis of a "Christian" nation. When we talk of building Christian nations we mean building nations whose foundational principles are Biblical. If they are, then the principles will be manifested in the nation's law base and in the societal institutions.

As we examine the following foundations, most of the application is in the civil realm. We could just as easily apply them to families, individual lives, businesses, and the church.

1. Self-Government

When people hear the word *government* they usually think of civil government for in most nations that is **the** government.

In a general sense *government* means *direction, regulation, control, restraint*. There are many spheres of government each providing direction, regulation, control, and restraint in its jurisdiction. The spheres of government can be divided into **internal** and **external** government. Another name for internal government is self-government. All government begins internally in the heart of man, with his ability to govern his conscience, will, character, thoughts, ideas, motives, conviction, attitudes, and desires. How a man governs himself internally affects his external actions, speech, conduct, use of property, etc. Each external sphere of government is a reflection of the internal sphere. In other words, the internal is causative to the external. The type of government that exists in the homes, churches, schools, businesses, associations, or civil realms of a country is a reflection of the self-government within the citizens.

The seventeenth century Dutch scholar, Hugo Grotius, who systematized the subject of the Law of Nations, summarized the principle of self-government in the following quote:

> *"He knows not how to rule a kingdom, that cannot manage a Province; nor can he wield a Province, that cannot order a City; nor he order a City, that knows not how to regulate a Village; nor he a Village, that cannot guide a Family; nor can that man Govern well a Family that knows not how to Govern himself; neither can any Govern himself unless his reason be Lord, Will and Appetite her Vassals; nor can Reason rule unless herself be ruled by God, and (wholly) be obedient to Him."* [2]

Stated another way, you must rule yourself before you can rule others. The Bible teaches that rulers must be self-governed. One quality of a church leader was that he *"manages his own household well, keeping his children under control with all dignity (but if a man does not know how to manage his own household, how will he take care of the church of God?)"* (1 Timothy 3:4-5).

There are many civil government leaders today who are attempting to govern their nation, yet are unable to effectively direct and control their own lives or their families. These men and women should be replaced by those who can rule their own lives. Those who are self-governed are the ones with real power according to the Bible: *"He who is slow to anger is better than the mighty, and he who rules his spirit, than he who captures a city"* (Proverbs 16:32).

Grotius' statement reveals how the flow of power should occur within a country, from the internal to the external. He speaks of decentralized governmental units wielding less power the further removed they are from the individual. The following chart summarizes his ideas:

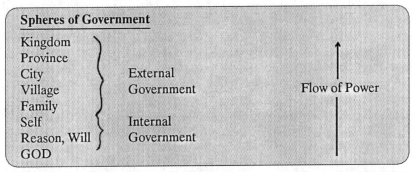

Effective government begins by an individual learning to govern himself. The more internal self-government a person possesses, the less external government he needs. Consequently, the more rules and laws required to keep people acting rightly is a revelation of a diminishing amount of self-government. History teaches that man can control himself, but only to a limited degree. Since self-government cannot be imposed externally, and man is limited in personal self-discipline, there needs to be another source for internal control. Grotius reveals that man can only be truly self-governed if his reason, will, and appetite are ruled by God. The basis of self-control is obedience to the Creator and His standards of conduct found in the Bible.

The fourth President of the United States and chief architect of the U.S. Constitution, James Madison, stated:

"We have staked the whole future of American civilization, not upon the power of government, far from it. We have staked the future of all our political institutions upon the capacity of mankind for self-government; upon the capacity of each and all of us to govern ourselves, to control ourselves, to sustain ourselves according to the Ten Commandments of God." [3]

As people in a nation become less self-governed, and give up power, the civil government (especially the national government) will grow and grow, making more and more laws (many outside its realm of jurisdiction) and spending more and more money. Lack of self-government leads to greater centralized external government which results in loss of individual liberty.

2. Union or Covenant

The people of a free nation will not only be self-governed but will also voluntarily work in union with each other for the common good of the entire nation.

Most of history reveals that civil unions were a result of centralization via political force and military might rather than voluntary consent. Christianity provided the basis of a "community united, not by external bonds, but by the vital force of distinctive ideas and principles."[4] Civil covenants started in America in 1620 when English Pilgrims drew up the Mayflower Compact. They were able to covenant to live together in civil society because some years earlier they had covenanted to join themselves together in a church estate. In fact, American constitutionalism (which has effected constitutions in most nations) is based upon the Biblical idea of covenant.

The Bible is full of covenants between man and man and between God and man. The covenant that God makes with men through the atoning work of Jesus Christ is the beginning of the internal heart change necessary for the foundation of freedom in an individual and in a nation. Biblical marriage covenants keep marriages together and strong. Without strong families, no nation can long endure.

The external union of a people results from an internal unity of ideas and principles residing in the hearts of the people. Compulsory union, that imposed by external force and fear, will never last. Union cannot be forced externally, but must arise from internal unity. An understanding of the foundations and framework of a free government must be inculcated in the hearts of all the people for a nation to remain together in union.

Covenant or compact among people on a local level is the basis of political union. For people to covenant together, they must share common beliefs, purposes, ideas, and faith. Joining together for civil purposes begins with covenanting together for independent purposes, such as in homes, churches, schools, clubs, and various organizations. Union is also seen in the commercial realm in partnerships and corporations. Independent and commercial unions not only benefit the people directly involved, but also the general populace. If there is not unity with union on the independent and commercial levels, there can be no political union.

Stronger internal bonds within a people will produce a stronger union. A people working together in union will bring a great increase to the strength of a country.

The application of the principle of union in the various levels of government will allow them to work together for the good of all, while self-government in the people will assure that the rights of individuals are maintained as well. The principles of self-government and union must be kept in balance. Too much emphasis on union will result in centralism, while too much emphasis on self-government leads to disintegration of the nation.

3. Individuality

The principle of individuality reveals that each person is created by God and is unique and distinct. Each has a well defined existence with unique talents and abilities which fits him for a special purpose. All men are alike in many ways (there is a unity among mankind), yet no two men are alike (there is also diversity). Man has physical characteristics that make him unique, such as his fingerprints, profile, voiceprints, scent, and nerve pattern on the inside of the eye. He also has unique internal characteristics, including thoughts, opinions, emotions, and attitudes.

Man is a reflection of his Creator, who is a unity (God is One), yet He is also diverse (God is a triune Being). God does not create carbon-copy molds of anything, whether humans, animals, trees, minerals, mountains, rivers, planets or stars. Everything He creates is unique and distinct, yet there is a unity among all things for God created them all.

Every person has his own outward and inward identity or individuality. Every person is responsible and accountable for his own choices and actions. For governments to be free, the people must assume this responsibility.

Man, being created by God with a unique existence, has an independent value. His value is not dependent upon his ability to contribute to the state. Man is of highest value and the state exists to serve man, rather than man serve the state. Man, therefore, is superior to the state. In a government that views the state as paramount, individuals' lives, liberty, and property will be in danger if they do not cooperate with or contribute to the state.

The principle of individuality further reveals that all men are equal. However, men are not equal in their talents and abilities, but they are equal in their right to life, liberty and the pursuit of acquiring property. Governments embodying false ideas of equality say men have an equal right to material possessions and thus try to distribute the wealth accordingly. All men have equal rights before the law. Governments exist in order to secure those rights.

A free government will keep a balance of unity with diversity. Too much emphasis on diversity leads to anarchy or freedom run wild. In such a state man will be self-centered, and lawlessness, license, and nihilism will be predominant. The resulting forms of government will run from anarchy to pure democracy.

Tyranny will result from an over-emphasis on unity. The rulers (or ruler) will center in on themselves and do as they please for their benefit or what they consider to be of benefit to the whole. The result is centralization of power and slavery and bondage to large groups of people. The forms of government that result from this mentality range from bureaucracy or collectivism (socialism, communism) to dictatorship. Here, the central government determines the rights and liberties of the people.

A balance of unity and diversity will produce liberty with order in a society and government by the consent of the governed. The resulting form of government will be a decentralized, democratic constitutional republic.

4. Property or Conscience

We will see in a later chapter that a free market economy is one aspect of the framework of a free and just government. The components of a free market economy -- private property rights, individual enterprise, and a free market -- flow from the principle of property in the lives of the people. A person's property is whatever he has exclusive right to possess and control. Property is first internal. A person's conscience is his most precious aspect of property because it tells him what is right and wrong in his actions. Each person in a free government must be a good steward of his conscience and keep it clear. By doing so, he will know what is right and wrong from within and, therefore, he will be able to live his life in a right manner. The apostle Paul said he did his "best to maintain always a blameless conscience both before God and before men" (Acts 24:16).

How one takes care of his internal property will determine how he takes care of his external property. The following chart reveals various aspects of internal and external property:

Internal Property	External Property
Thoughts	Land/Estate
Opinions	Money
Talents	Freedom of Speech
Conscience	Bodily Health
Ideas	Possessions
Mind	Freedom of Assembly
Affections	

Governments exist to protect property of every sort, most importantly, liberty of conscience. Tyrannical governments will invade rights of conscience as well as external property rights. The power that can invade liberty of conscience, can also usurp civil liberty. Internal property rights must, therefore, be guarded at all costs, for as they are diminished, every inalienable right of man is jeopardized.

The famous British political scientist, John Locke, wrote in his treatise *Of Civil Government:*

"For Men being the Workmanship of one Omnipotent, and infinitely wise

Maker: All the Servants of one Sovereign Master, sent into the World by His Order, and about His Business, they are His Property, whose Workmanship they are, made to last during His, not one anothers Pleasure..." [5]

Locke goes on to state that while we are God's property, God has given us the responsibility to be good stewards over our persons. He wrote that *"every man has a Property in his own Person."* It follows we have a God-given right to everything necessary to preserve our persons, to internal and external property.

In other words, God has created everything, including us, and given us the right to possess internal and external property. God requires us to be good stewards of everything He puts into our hand, whether that be houses, land, and money or talents, abilities, and knowledge. The idea of stewardship is embodied in the principle of property.

Before any property can be taken from us, we must give our consent. If our property can be taken without our consent, then we really have no property. This is why any taxes imposed by a government on its citizens must be done by elected representatives. We give our consent to taxes or laws affecting our property rights through our representatives. If they do not represent our views, we should work to replace them in a lawful manner.

A people standing on the principle of property will take action to prohibit government or other citizens from taking anyone's personal property without their consent, or from violating anyone's conscience and rights. Lack of this principle in the lives of citizens will lead to unjust taxation, a government controlled economy, and usurpation of both internal and external property rights.

5. Education - Sowing and Reaping

An ignorant people will quickly become a people enslaved. Only a well-instructed citizenry can be permanently free. To preserve liberty in a nation, the general populace must understand the principles upon which a free government is based, for as they do, they will be able to prevent the leaders from eroding their Constitutional rights and protections.

Education is a sowing and reaping process. It is like a seed. The Bible tells us much about the "seed principle." It is extremely important for us to understand the parable of the sower and the soils (Mark 4), and that the kingdom of God is like a seed. Although we are instantly converted when we repent and submit ourselves to Christ, the establishment of God's character and kingdom within us is a gradual process. It takes place like the growth of a plant or tree. A seed is planted; nourishment, care, and sunlight are provided; and then a mature plant comes forth bearing fruit (we must remember the pruning process, also).

This same principle applies in establishing God's truth in the nations of the world. It is a gradual process that must occur in one way through Christian education.

The ideas that are sown in a people will grow over the years and produce fruit, manifesting in every aspect of life -- personal, social, political, economic. That is why the philosophy of the schools in one generation will be the philosophy of government in the next.

What the educational institutions of a country teach lays the foundation for liberty or bondage, depending upon the ideas imparted. Education is the means for propagating a governmental philosophy. In recent years, where Marxists have taken over certain countries, one of the first things they have done is to assume control of the educational system and through that teach their ideologies and propagate their ideas.

Each form of government has its own philosophy of education. Public educational institutions will always teach the philosophy of the government of the state. This is one reason why most education should be kept in the private sector. Any governmental or public schools should be decentralized and controlled on the local level. If the educational philosophy of a nation is changed, the governmental philosophy will change in the future.

For a free government to be sustained the people must have an understanding of the working and structure of free government. The people can then keep an enlightened eye on their civil leaders. However, education involves more than just acquiring knowledge or learning facts. Of greater importance is education in morals and principles. We have seen that the citizens of a nation that desire to be free and prosperous must be people of principle. Education in the Christian religion and morality is of first importance. Such education should not merely impart knowledge of morality, but actually implant morals and virtue within the people. The Godly characteristics that are almost universally accepted as fundamental for societies all have their roots in the Bible. These include honesty, loyalty, concern for others, diligence and many more.

13

True education is the means for propagating free government to future generations. Without it, tyranny will reign.

6. Morality or Christian Character

No nation can long endure without virtue or morality in the people. A loss of principles and manners is the greatest threat to a free people and will cause its downfall more surely than any foreign enemy. Samuel Adams, the father of the American Revolution, said, "while the people are virtuous they cannot be subdued; but when once they lose their virtue they will be ready to surrender their liberties to the first external or internal invader."[6] He went on to say that the greatest security from enslavement in a country is virtue or morality among the people.

Everyone's fundamental rights are threatened by a lack of morality in the people. People of character will desire to observe the law and will not willfully take the life, liberty or property of others. Consequently, people will not live in fear of other citizens. In addition, less government will be required in a virtuous nation. Since fewer people will violate the law, a large police force and judicial system will not be needed. Law making bodies will also have less to do because prohibitive laws will be at a minimum, as citizens will constrain themselves.

In a virtuous nation the rulers will be moral. This produces more freedom because the rulers will not usurp individual rights through bad legislation and they will not steal from people through fiat money, excessive or graduated taxes, or other means. Consequently, people will not live in fear of civil government.

What is virtue or character? Virtue has been defined as a conformity to a standard of right, and also a voluntary obedience to truth. Character is a convictional belief that results in consistent behavior.

Character literally means "to stamp and engrave through pressure." This sums up nicely what God is doing in our lives. God's plan is to make each person like Him. Romans 8:29 tells us that God has predestined that we, as His children, are to be conformed into the image of Christ. He is building His character within us, or you might say He is stamping and engraving upon us His image. He is doing this so that we might be examples of Him to the world and, also, that we may be able to fulfill His purpose for our lives.

14

History has shown that virtue and character in a people is the basis of happiness in a society and is absolutely necessary for a state to long remain free. As human nature is corrupted, the foundations of freedom are easily destroyed.

Following are some characteristics of virtuous citizens:

- They will have a concern for the common good above their own self-interest.
- They will vigorously participate in local, regional, and national government, and will seek to correct wrong conduct in public officials.
- If necessary, they will risk their life, fortune, and honor for their country.
- They will perform their duties and seek to have right conduct in public and private.

A free market economy is dependent upon the people being virtuous because such a people:

- Will not steal from their employees or others. Such theft increases the cost of goods and services for everyone.
- Will have a strong work ethic and be productive. This hard labor will cause the economy to grow.
- Will respect contracts.
- Will save and invest to acquire a greater return later.
- Will have a concern for their posterity and will seek to pass on a greater estate than they received.
- Will not waste public resources and will be good stewards of the environment.

Therefore, a lack of character in the people can produce the following: a stagnant or declining economy, corrupt laws, a lack of smooth transition from one political leader or party to another after elections, a corrupt military that may take control of the government, and increased power in civil government to attempt to solve the many problems that result from lack of character in the people.

A virtuous people will be vigilant to work to establish a free nation and then also to maintain it. Eternal vigilance is the price to maintain liberty. People of character will be eternally vigilant to secure their rights and demand that their government's power remain limited.

7. Faith in God and His Word

The foundational principles (and, as we shall see, the framework) of a free society flow directly or indirectly out of the faith or religion of the people. The principles we have just examined all come from the Bible. Each one of these principles, which must be a part of people's lives for a free nation to be established and maintained, require the indispensable support of the Creator.

With the principle of individuality, we saw that the uniqueness and value of man comes from his being created by God. Man becomes self-governing as he is subject to God and His truth. Morality cannot exist separate from religion. Man's most precious possession, his conscience, responds to right or wrong put in his heart by his Creator. The strongest force to bring union between a people is a common faith. Education that will propagate liberty must sow seeds of truth. All truth originates with God.

For the fundamental rights of man to be secure from government, the people must recognize that these rights are endowed by their Creator, and not granted by government. If people think that government, or man, is the source of rights then government can take away the rights of the people. But if God gives rights to men, then they are inalienable.

To secure liberty for all men, the answer to the following question must be understood: "Who is the source of law in a society?" In reality, the source of law in a society is the god of that society. If man is the final source of the law, then the law will constantly change as man's ideas and understanding changes. God is the source of true law and His law is absolute. William Blackstone, the great English legal scholar, said that no human laws are of any validity, if contrary to the higher law of God.

In studying the development of individual and civil liberty, it is readily apparent that the Christian faith has provided laws that have produced the greatest amount of freedom and prosperity in history.

Christianity has produced the power or principles in the people necessary to support liberty. Certain aspects of this law of liberty are revealed to all men, in what Blackstone called the Laws of Nature. However, the primary way that God has revealed His law to man is through the Bible, the written word of God. To the degree that nations have applied the principles of the Bible, is the degree to which those nations have prospered and been free. The author of the first exhaustive dictionary, Noah Webster, stated:

> *"Almost all the civil liberty now enjoyed in the world owes its origin to the principles of the Christian religion...The religion which has introduced civil liberty, is the religion of Christ and his apostles, which enjoins humility, piety, and benevolence; which acknowledges in every person a brother, or a sister, and a citizen with equal rights. This is genuine Christianity, and to this we owe our free constitutions of government...."* [7]

Every nation is based upon some religion. Christianity brings, not only individual, but also civil liberty.

Power and Form of Free Government

External forms always result from an internal power. This is true for civil governments, churches, homes, businesses, or associations. The power, which is internal, precedes the form, which is external.

Both a power and a form are needed for anything to function properly. The internal power is the life or energizing force and is essential for any form to work as it should; yet, a form is absolutely necessary to channel the power properly. We not only need power and form, but we also need a balance between the two. Too much form causes all involved to dry up, while too much power causes them to "blow up." Communism, for example, produces a form of civil government that relies almost totally on external pressure to keep everyone "in line." The internal creativity, life, and motivation of each individual is suppressed and often dries up by these external constraints. An over-emphasis on power leads to anarchy and eventually bondage. Historically, this can be seen after many national revolutions, the French being an excellent example.

In later chapters we will examine the form of a free government, a free economy, and other external aspects of free nations. The principles examined in this section reveal the power of a free nation. The form of a free government, free economy, etc. can only come forth and be maintained by a people that have the proper power or spirit within them. Without this foundation, a free government can never be established or maintained. It is not enough for a nation to copy some external form of government to secure liberty. That external form must flow out of the principles of liberty within the heart of the people. The pathway to liberty within a nation is from the internal to the external.

These principles make a strong foundation which provides a proper support for individuals, families, churches, associations, and governments enabling them to withstand any pressure and build a society that is free, just, prosperous, peaceful, and long-lasting.

Chapter 2

God's Plan for the Nations

Both Christians and non-Christians throughout history have recognized that Christianity provides the foundation needed for free nations. Benjamin Franklin said: *"He who shall introduce into public affairs the principles of primitive Christianity will change the face of the world."* [1]

One goal of this book is to equip Christians to be able to introduce Biblical principles into public affairs, and in so doing bring Godly change throughout the world. As we learn to operate nations on Biblical principles, we will be participating in bringing liberty to the world and hence helping to fulfill part of God's plan for the nations.

The Need for World Reformation

The Bible reveals to us that the world longs for liberation. Romans 8:19,21 says that *"... creation eagerly waits for the revealing of the sons of God... because creation itself also will be delivered from the bondage of corruption into the glorious liberty of the children of God"* (NKJV). The following statistics show the desperate need for real answers to world problems:

"(1.)Megapoverty - 2.1 billion people (46% of world) live in poverty, of whom 800 million live in absolute poverty; 1.1 billion without adequate shelter, 2.1 billion without adequate water supply, 3 billion with unsafe water and bad sanitation, 800 million adults illiterate, 850 million with no access to schools, 1.5 billion with no access to medical care, 500 million on edge of starvation (20 million starvation-related deaths a year), 1.5 billion hungry or malnourished.

"(2.)Abortion - 75% of world's population live in countries where abortion is legal, though regarded by most Christians as murder; 25% of all pregnancies worldwide end in abortion, resulting in 65 million abortions a year of which 38% are illegal.

"(3.)Military coups - Armed forces' takeovers of governments escalate to over 50% of world's countries.

"(4.)Debt - Third World owes First World more than $1 trillion; corporate debt exceeds $1.5 trillion; possibility of global crash imminent.

"(5.)Human rights - Increasing vulnerability of human rights; widespread government use of torture, increasing from 98 countries in 1980 to 110 countries, especially in South America (Colombia, Peru, Paraguay, Chile), Africa and Asia (Syria, Pakistan, Iran, etc.).

"(6.)Refugees - World total of refugees of all kinds in asylum countries fluctuates around 20 million from 1965 to 1987.

"(7.)Megacrime - International crime now costs $400 billion a year; megafraud and computer crime $44 billion; illegal hard drug industry and traffic $110 billion, representing 38% of all organized crime; includes 25 million cocaine users in USA ($25 billion), 60 million marijuana users....

"(8.)Totalitarian Governments - The number of citizens killed by totalitarian or extreme authoritarian governments reaches 130 million since 1900 (1918-53, USSR kills 40 million citizens, China under Mao 45 million, 1975-79 Cambodia 2 million, et alia), far greater than 36 million combatants killed in wars since 1900; absolutist governments now mankind's deadliest scourge." [2]

The Answers Are Found in the Bible

We saw in Chapter 1 that the truth of the Bible provides mankind with principles of liberty that bring real freedom to those individuals and nations who are oppressed. God created the earth and from the beginning gave man the responsibility to rule over it. Genesis 1:28 says: *"And God blessed them; and God said to them, 'Be fruitful and multiply, and fill the earth and subdue it; and rule over... the earth.' "* When man rejected God's Law, and lost the ability to not only govern himself, but also to govern society, public tyranny and oppression reigned through sinful men.

Through the ministry and death of Jesus Christ, however, the power for both self- and civil government was restored to mankind. Though internal liberty was a primary focus of Jesus Christ, it must not be overlooked that His inaugural and farewell sermons both emphasized external civil liberty. In Luke 4:18, Christ's first public message focused on *"liberty"* for *"the poor... the captives... [and] those who are oppressed..."* It is safe to assume that poverty, slavery, tyranny and injustice were on the Lord's mind when, in His final sermon, He commissioned His followers to *"Go therefore and make disciples of all the nations..."* (Matthew 28:19). The great Bible commentator Matthew Henry explains that *"the principal intention of this commission"* is clear. It is to *"... do your utmost to make the nations Christian nations."* This is God's plan for the nations.

The apostle Paul understood this plan very well and sought to communicate it to the Christians of the first century. In 1 Corinthians 6:2 Paul asks a vital question: *"Do you not know that the Christians will one day judge and govern the world?"* (Amplified Bible). If this is true, Paul says, then they ought to at least be competent to hold public offices such as the local judgeships in Greece. To those Christians in Corinth, as well as in the world today, who incorrectly assume that Paul means we should rule **only** in the next age after the second coming of Christ, the next question and answer of the apostle is aimed: *"Do you not know that we shall judge angels? How much more the matters of this life?"* (vs. 3). Paul then rebukes the Christians for their apathy and irresponsibility that allowed non-Christians to be in control: *"If then you have law courts dealing with matters of this life, do you appoint them as judges who are of no account in the church. I say this to your shame"* (vs. 4-5).

This shameful situation has become the reality in nations today. The battle for God's earth (Psalm 24:1) is being lost today mainly because Christians have thought that God does not really care about such things. They fail to see that Christ taught us to focus our prayers, not on heaven, but upon His kingdom coming *"on earth as it is in heaven"* (Matthew 6:9,10). The results of such ignorance and neglect of duty has been costly in the 20th century.

Nations throughout the world have not been presented with a true Biblical theology of liberty and so are being increasingly deceived by Satan's counterfeit philosophies. One is "Liberation Theology" which incorrectly identifies the root of public evil as the socio-economic environment, and claims that liberation comes through violent revolution, followed by the people's dependency on a government they can trust. Christ, in contrast, says the root of evil is the heart of man, and therefore, external liberty is possible only when it flows from the internal to the external. Revival therefore must precede reformation.

Jesus Christ spoke of this "cause and effect" principle in Luke 6:43-45:

> *"For there is no good tree which produces bad fruit; nor, on the other hand, a bad tree which produces good fruit. For each tree is known by its own fruit;... The good man out of the good treasure of his heart brings forth what is good; and the evil man out of the evil treasure of his heart brings forth what is evil."*

Every effect has a cause. The fruit is determined by the root. Man's conduct is determined by man's heart. The external is determined by the internal. All external "forms" or structures come from some internal "power." This is the principle of Power and Form mentioned in Chapter 1. The Christian religion is the essential power needed to create and preserve a form of government that is free and just.

History is Shaped By the Heart of Man Under the Providence of God

The external affairs of a nation are a reflection of the condition of the hearts of the people. French Historian Charles Rollin reflects the view of most eighteenth century writers in stating that God is sovereign over history, but deals with nations dependent upon the heart and action of the people. He wrote:

> *"Nothing gives history a greater superiority to many branches of literature, than to see in a manner imprinted, in almost every page of it, the precious footsteps and shining proofs of this great truth, viz. that God disposes all events as Supreme Lord and Sovereign; that He alone determines the fate of kings and the duration of empires; and that he transfers the government of kingdoms from one nation to another because of the unrighteous dealings and wickedness committed therein."* [3]

You cannot understand history without understanding Divine Providence. George Bancroft, eminent historian of American history in the 19th century said, *"Providence is the light of history and the soul of the world. God is in history and all history has a unity because God is in it."* Providential history is true history. Many modern educators deny the Providential view of history and would have us believe that their promotion of one of several "secular" views of history is simply the recounting of brute facts. They fail to tell their students that their own humanistic presuppositions and religious doctrines determine their choice of people, places, principles, and events. They fail to communicate that neutrality is not possible in the teaching of history, for the historian's world-view will dictate his perspective. Even as there are not many interpretations of Scripture (2 Pet. 1:20, 21), neither are there of history -- there is really only one correct view; that which is the Author's interpretation and perspective. God is the Author of Scripture and History.

Reverend S.W. Foljambe, in 1876, defined history as *"the autobiography of Him 'who worketh all things after the counsel of His will' (Eph. 1:11) and who is graciously timing all events after the counsel of His Christ, and the Kingdom of God on earth. It is His-Story."* [4]

The Bible overwhelmingly affirms this truth. Let us examine just a few Scriptures along this line:

Acts 17:24-26 - *"The God who made the world... gives to all life and breath and all things; and He made... every nation..., having determined their appointed times, and the boundaries of their habitation..."*

1 Timothy 6:15-16 - *"He is the blessed and only Sovereign, the King of Kings and Lord of lords;... To Him be honor and eternal dominion! Amen."*

Proverbs 16:9-10 - *"The mind of man plans his way, but the Lord directs his steps. A divine decision is in the lips of the king."*

Job 12:23 - *"He makes the nations great, then destroys them; He enlarges the nations, then leads them away."*

Psalms 22:28 - *"For the kingdom is the Lord's, and He rules over the nations."*

Daniel 2:21 - *"It is He who changes the times and the epochs; He removes kings and establishes kings."*

Daniel 4:17, 26 - *"The Most High is ruler over the realm of mankind;... Your kingdom will be assured to you after you recognize it is Heaven that rules."*

A beginning point in liberating any nation is for the citizens to see and acknowledge the providence of God in their past, present, and future. In his original dictionary published in 1828 Noah Webster defines "Providence" as *"the care and superintendence which God exercises over His creatures."*

It is vital that a nation learns of its Providential history. Rev. A.W. Foljambe warns that, *"the more thoroughly a nation deals with its history, the more decidedly will it recognize and own an over-ruling Providence therein, and the more religious a nation it will become; while the more superficially it deals with its history, seeing only secondary causes and human agencies, the more irreligious will it be."*[5]

A lack of providential education, especially of God as the author of history, contributes as much as any other factor to the rise of secularism in a nation.

Providential Geography

"And He made from one, every nation of mankind to live on all the face of the earth, having determined their appointed times, and the boundaries of their habitation." (Acts 17:26)

God is not only sovereign in the historical development of nations -- He made every nation, and determined when they would exist -- but He also has determined their boundaries.

God's plan for the nations has been unfolding in a specific geographic direction. This geographical march of history is called the **Chain of Christianity** or the **Chain of Liberty**.[6] Another way to define the **Chain of Liberty** is the sequence of events in the lives of men and nations that are links or stepping stones in history which result in bringing forth internal **and** external liberty, both personal and civil liberty.

The Bible attests to this geographical march of the Gospel:

"And they passed through the Phrygian and Galatian region, having been forbidden by the Holy Spirit to speak the word in Asia; and when they had come to Mysia, they were trying to go into Bithynia, and the Spirit of Jesus

did not permit them; and passing by Mysia, they came down to Troas. And a vision appeared to Paul in the night: a certain man of Macedonia was standing and appealing to him and saying, 'Come over to Macedonia and help us.' And when he had seen the vision, immediately we sought to go into Macedonia, concluding that God had called us to preach the gospel to them" (Acts 16:6-10).

Why did God forbid Paul to speak the word in Asia? It is because He had other plans for the spread of the gospel. Paul and his companions were trying to go into Bithynia (northeast of where they were in Mysia) to preach the word, but God called them west into Europe. This was not by chance, but by God's choice in accordance with His plan for reaching the world with the gospel. From the beginning God has had a systematic plan for filling the earth with his glory.

We know from later Biblical events (see for example Romans 15:19,28 -- Illyricum is the Baltic region of Europe) and world history that the spread of Christianity (and hence civilization) has occurred in a westward direction. It is true that early disciples carried the gospel into Northern Africa and in much of Asia, but it was in Europe where Christianity firmly took root and affected the entire society. As we will see, Christianity produced internal and external liberty in a westward direction. This is why we speak of the westward move of the Chain of Christianity.

Each continent and nation has a unique destiny or purpose, as well as a unique geographic structure. The study of a nation's or continent's geographic individuality -- its unique placement on the earth in relation to the other continents, its unique geographic structure, coastline, and climate, and its unique people groups -- in conjunction with it's history, certainly reveals the sovereignty of God over the nations.

The Individuality of the Continents

Like Europe, God has prepared all the continents for a specific purpose. Insight into the purpose of a continent or nation can be revealed by studying its geographic structure.

What is geography? The word "geography" is derived from two greek words meaning "the earth" and "to write". We could figuratively say that geography is God's handwriting on the earth. He is the only one who is big enough to write on the earth!

"Christian" geography (which is true geography) is the view that the earth's origin, end, purposes, and physiography (physical structure, climate, plant and animal distribution) are for Christ and His glory.

Shakespeare was correct in saying that "all the world's a stage." God is the One who has created the props, placing the mountains, oceans, rivers, seas, deserts, islands, and continents just where He wanted them in order that they might assist in carrying out His plan for mankind on the earth.

God's Principle of Individuality

In examining the principle of Individuality in Chapter 1 we saw that all of God's creation is a reflection of his infinity, diversity, and individuality. God does not create carbon-copy entities, but distinct and unique individualities, be they animals, plants, humans, planets, stars, etc. While a unity exists among all creation, since all is created by God, there also exists a great diversity, since God himself is three, yet one. God displays the principle of individuality, and his creation does as well.

People display the principle of individuality.

There are certain characteristics that all humans have (unity), yet no two people are alike (diversity):
- Each person has a unique purpose and call from God.
- Each person also has unique characteristics, both internal and external.

One external characteristic that you possess that no one else has are your fingerprints. Of the five billion people on the earth today, no two have the same fingerprints. You also have a unique profile, voiceprints, and nerve pattern on the inside of your eye. Internal characteristics that are uniquely yours include your thoughts, attitudes, and emotions. These are just a few characteristics you possess that reveal that God made you "the one and only you".

God gives us certain internal and external characteristics that enable us to fulfill our God-given purpose and call. (As an example, God made Eric Liddell physically fast so that he could win races and bring God glory through it.)

Nations also display God's principle of individuality.

Like individuals, nations have a unique purpose. As an example, Babylon was used by God to bring his judgement upon Israel by taking them into captivity. We will see throughout this book how God has raised up and put down nations of the world for his purposes.

Nations also have unique characteristics, such as their time of existence in history, their power, national spirit, geographic location, boundaries, and structure. As with people, God gives nations unique characteristics in order that they can fulfill their divine purposes in history.

Chapter 3

Origins & Development of Government & Liberty

Self-government and Family Government

The history of government and of civil liberty begins in the Garden of Eden with the first man. God placed man in the Garden and gave him a Dominion Mandate to subdue and rule all creatures, which included man governing himself (Genesis 1:26-28). All government therefore begins with the individual; power flows from the individual to the other spheres of life. The test of man's self-government in the beginning was his ability to resist eating of the forbidden tree without any type of external restraints. He had to internally govern himself according to God's Creation Law in order to succeed (Genesis 2:16-17). Creation Law is also known as the "Law of Nature" (Romans 1:18-20;2:14-15; it did not originate in Greek thought). The Law of Nature was supplemented later by the "Law of Nature's God," i.e. the revealed Law of God in the Bible. The Law of Nature is summed up succinctly in the Golden Rule (Matt 7:12) and in the command to "love your neighbor as yourself" (Gal 5:14). The Moral Law (Creation Law), which all men know by nature, differs from the ceremonial and political law delivered by Moses. The political and ceremonial law must be taught or preached in order to be known (Rom 1:16; 10:14-17).

Through Adam's failure to control himself, sin entered into the world and made it difficult for any man to govern himself. At this time no civil government had been established. The Dominion Mandate initially given to Adam did not include the responsibility for ruling over other men. Therefore, when Cain did not control his anger and jealousy, and he violently slew his brother, who do we see taking responsibility for justice and protection? God Himself (Genesis 4:1-16). God did establish family government in the beginning.

The Bible reveals that from ancient times the responsibilities of every individual. They include: worship, work and charity. The responsibilities of the family include: Reproduction, Education, Health and Welfare, and transferral of inheritance.

Civil Government for Protection

After a period of time the prevalence of sin and lack of self-government led to so much violence that God saw the end result would be all men destroying one another (Genesis 6:5-13). Therefore, God decided to intervene and bring a flood to destroy all but one righteous family. When God brought Noah through the flood to a new earth, He re-established the Cultural Mandate, but modified it by delegating to man the responsibility for governing other men in order to protect innocent human life from sinful, violent men (Gen 9:5-7). He does this by instituting capital punishment--the backbone of civil government.

Civil government, then, is just as much a Divine institution as the Family and the Church. It was established by God on the premise that men are sinners and human life is sacred and valuable. It was established with clear purposes and principles of operation revealed in Scripture. Here are some scriptures defining the purpose of civil government:

> *"Submit yourselves for the Lord's sake to every human institution, whether to a king as the one in authority, or to governors as sent by him for the punishment of evildoers and the praise of those who do right." (1 Peter 2:13-14)*

> *"Let every person be in subjection to the governing authorities;...For rulers are not a cause of fear for good behavior, but for evil;...for it is a minister of God to you for good. But if you do what is evil, be afraid;...for it is a minister of God, an avenger who brings wrath upon the one who practices evil." (Romans 13:1,3,4)*

30

The purpose of government, therefore, is to protect the life, liberty, and property of all individuals by punishing evildoers and encouraging the righteous. It is to insure domestic tranquility, secure liberty, and provide for the common defense (1 Tim 2:1,2). When governing rulers ever fail to do this, then they themselves are resisting the ordinances of God and are illegitimate authorities who should be resisted and replaced.

The main functions of the Family, church, and civil government can be summarized as procreation, propagation, and protection respectively. Most Christians today may know much about the first two Divine institutions, but very little about the latter. Just one walk through a common Christian bookstore shows the lack of material on this subject, although the Bible deals with it abundantly.

Civil government functioned in a patriarchal/tribal fashion for a long time. Noah was the first patriarch, i.e. a civil ruler of a family group who ruled by a covenant relationship. Under the patriarch were elders, i.e. aged senators, who led each tribe (Gen. 10:21; 50:7; 2 Sam. 12:17; Heb. 11:2). Eventually, as they built cities (Gen 10:5), the elders would meet and govern at the gates of the city (Deut. 21:2-6; 19:12,21,22,25).

Ancient Asian and African Culture

In Genesis 10:4,20,31,32 we find the first reference to "nations" arising from family groups. We also find the rise of pagan monarchy (kingdoms) as the form of civil government in these nations. Centralization of power is a pagan tendency and was also seen in the rise of the first city-states, such as at Nineveh (Genesis 10:11) and then Babel (Genesis 11:1). Noah's great grandson, Nimrod, the founder of Nineveh, was the first "mighty one" or dictator in the earth (he was also known as king Sargon). Mesopotamian culture (c.3000) was dominated first by the Sumerians, followed by the Babylonians and the Assyrians. Egypt (c.3200) with its "Pharaohs" is mentioned in Genesis 12:10, 15. Nine kings are mentioned in Genesis 14:1,2 which shows the pagan centralization that was true also of ancient Crete, India, China, and Andean culture.

Nowhere in Scripture is civil government said to have responsibility to be provider or savior for men by the centralization of its of powers; yet, the men at Babel began to congregate together for this goal rather than spread out and "fill the earth" (Gen 1:28). They wanted to make a name for themselves and save themselves through the state as their *counterfeit* Messiah. This was the first public expression of humanism where sovereignty was placed in a man or a collection of men rather than God (Genesis 11:1-8). In order to prevent centralized, one-world government, God made diverse languages (which are an effective deterrent to this day) and dispersed the various races, tribes and nations across the globe (c.2300).

All nations therefore are a result of God's creative act, not only in ancient times but throughout history. Paul the apostle said that God determines the duration and boundaries of every nation on earth (Acts 17:26).

The Hebrew Republic with Biblical Civil Laws

In the midst of this centralizing corruption of the Divine institution of government, God called a man named Abraham (c. 2166-1991 B.C.) who lived in the city-state of Ur (which was confederated with Babel, Nineveh, and Accad), to begin a unique "nation" as a model among the pagan nations (Genesis 11:31; 12:1-3; 17:6,10; 18:19; 22:18). Abraham became a godly "prince" (Genesis 23:6) or ruler of Israel and taught that: (1) the world is governed by the fixed laws of the One God, not by the whims of a multitude of prankish gods; and (2) the self-governing family, based on covenantal ideas that began with Noah, is the basis of freedom and order. Abraham negotiated and battled with Pharaoh (Genesis 12:18), kings of Sodom and Salem (Genesis 14:17,18), and the King of Gerar (Genesis 20:2 and 21:27) as he struggled to birth a nation that would bless the world by its example.

Under Joseph's leadership the Hebrews migrated into Egypt to survive a famine and ended up becoming slaves. Then God raised up a man named Moses (1526-1406), who was a Hebrew but grew up in the house of the Egyptian royal family, to liberate his people from slavery. After becoming a free people once again, God led Moses to organize their laws and form of government (Ex. 4:29; Ps. 107:32). The first representative republic on earth was established.

The Laws of Moses were unique in ancient history, quite different from the Laws of Hammurabi of Babylon made about 200 years earlier. They were much more humane, equitable , merciful, and respectful of the rights of women and slaves. The Decalogue or Ten Commandments (Ex 20:2-17) are explained by the Book of the Covenant (Ex 20:22-23:33). [Case laws are found in Ex. 21:1-22, 17; General laws in Ex. 22:18-23, 33]. The first four commandments are further expounded in the Holiness Code (Lev. 17-27). The latter six commandments are more deeply explained in the Deuteronomic Code (Deut. 12-26). The Decalogue provided for the protection of ten valuable things which, therefore, are "rights." A right is a just claim upon an express command of God, or in accordance with His will.

The Decalogue:

Prohibited:	Affirmed the Sanctity (or right) of:
1. Polytheism	God (sovereignty)
2. Idolatry	Worship
3. Profanity	Speech (vows)
4. Work on Sabbath	Time (rest)
5. Dishonor of Parents	Authority (family)
6. Murder	Life (individual)
7. Adultery	Love (contract)
8. Theft	Property
9. Perjury	Truth (reputation)
10. Coveting	Conscience

From the beginning, God's purpose was not limited to Israel, but He desired that these laws and their blessings might be exported to all nations on earth who had perverted God's plan of civil government into pagan, centralized monarchy.

God established in Israel seven crucial elements of free government:

1. A bicameral national legislature where one house was composed of elected judges or officers selected on the basis of population, not tribal groups (10s, 50s, 100s and 1,000s)(Dt. 1:13-17, Ex. 18:12-26).

2. A second house in the legislature was composed of two hereditary elders from eleven tribes or geographic areas (Ex. 24:1; Num. 11:16,17), plus the 24 priests from the tribe of Levi, plus 2 scribes/lawyers from each of all 12 tribes. This unelected body totaled 70 men and became known as the Sanhedrin.

3. A chief executive (Judge) elected by consent of the people and unable to exercise power without entering a covenant with the governed (1 Chr 11:3; Deut 17:14-20) in contrast to the pagan monarchs of the time.

4. A written "constitution" (covenant) (Ex. 19:5-8; 20:2-17). All of their civil laws were based upon God's higher fixed law, and not majorities. This makes it a republic, not a democracy.

5. A civilian militia and police force. (Deut 20:9,10 asserts the right to self-defense.)

6. An independent judiciary and fair trial (2 Chr 19:5-10; Ex. 23:1-3; Deut 17:6; Lev 20). [Deut 19:15-19 asserts: (1) that one is innocent until proven guilty, (2) the right to due process of law, (3) that one cannot be forced to testify against oneself, (4) accusers must personally confront you, (5) that judges must be impartial.]

7. A separation of the three branches of government (Isa 33:22) (Israel had a separate executive, judiciary, and legislature.)

Besides all of these structures, Israel also kept the government out of the areas properly under the jurisdiction of the individual, the family and the "church". Religion, the market, the press, and the schools were not control-led by the state. The priests and the Levites were the "clergy" and the judges of Israel were civil rulers. It is important to note that the "prophets" were primarily social reformers and statesmen among the people and included both clergy and non-clergy in their ranks. Separation of church and state, then, did not prohibit priests and Levites from holding public office or influencing politics as private citizens (Deut 17:8-13; 2 Chr 19:8,11).

The Hebrew people were governed by the elders after Joshua (Moses' successor) died without any chief executive to succeed him (Jos. 24:31), and at times showed great dependence on God, such as when Jephthah appealed to God to judge during a conflict with the Ammonites (Jud 11:27). However, they began to neglect the things that produced their character and philosophy of life. These were essential to support the Godly government established under Moses and the law. Gradually, the Family and Church deteriorated, which led to the corruption of Israel's government by 1120 B.C. New rulers came to power who were inept and unethical, and thus the people demanded a change. Unfortunately the change they chose was to demand a change in the government structure, instead of recognizing that the problem was one of the spirit and of internal character rather than of the letter of the

34

law. They asked for a king, which was a change from a decentralized, self-governing republic to a Constitutional Monarchy. This desire for a king to be like all the pagan nations around them (the pagans had no constitution, however) was rebuked by the prophet Samuel, but to no avail. Pagan monarchy would be effective in keeping order, but at the high price of oppression, taxation, and the loss of much liberty (1 Samuel 8:10-20). Israel conformed to this pagan form of civil government where dominion was turned into domination.

Centralizing power may solve the problems of the immediate but always leads to more problems down the road (1 Sam 8:1-22). From this point forward until the establishment of America -- almost 3000 years -- the entire world would know nothing of full external liberty for the individual man.

Greek and Roman Government

The second major attempt at democratic government in history was in the Greek city-states. Just about 60 years after Israel asked for a king (i.e. centralized government), Athens adopted a primitive type of democratic assembly and laws. Then in 884 B.C. the city-state of Sparta adopted the laws of Lycurgus and established a Senate. But the real era of democracy in Greece began in 598 B.C. when the Athenian lawgiver, Solon, drew up a legal system that would allow the people to make their own laws. Plato and Aristotle emphasized that a just society was one where every man is moved by concern for the common good.

The Greek democratic efforts finally collapsed around 405 B.C., but their concepts were embraced by Roman statesmen such as Cicero and Seneca in the second century before Christ. They proposed an impartial system of laws based on Natural Law which, Cicero said, comes from God and originated before "any written law existed or any state had been established."

The Greek and Roman theories were never as democratic as the Hebrew, however, because of their belief in inequality of men. The ideas of democracy and freedom were only extended to certain classes and all others were denied basic rights. Such tyranny eventually produced conflicts in society that led to chaos and disorder. Cicero was murdered and they reverted to complete totalitarianism to restore order. Greek and Roman contributions to democratic ideas were, therefore, more theoretical than actual, but were helpful to later generations who learned from their mistakes.

The fundamental flaws of their attempts at democracy were rooted in their belief that man was naturally unequal and that only one or a privileged few were competent to govern the rest.

The pagan and Christian ideas of man and government are contrasted well by American Historian Richard Frothingham. Of this pagan view that dominated the world at this time in history, he wrote:

> *"At that time, social order rested on the assumed natural inequality of men. The individual was regarded as of value only as he formed a part of the political fabric, and was able to contribute to its uses, as though it were the end of his being to aggrandize the State. This was the pagan idea of man. The wisest philosophers of antiquity could not rise above it. Its influence imbued the pagan world;...especially the idea that man was made for the State, the office of which, or of a divine right vested in one, or in a privileged few, was to fashion the thought and control the action of the many."* [1]

Pagan cultures condoned slavery and cruelty toward inferiors and exhibited no sympathy for the poor and suffering.

Jesus Christ Introduces the Christian Idea of Man and Government, A.D. 30

With the coming of Jesus Christ and His death on the cross for the sins of the world, man's ability to govern himself internally was restored. In addition to this internal liberty, Christ also proposed principles for external civil liberty. He clearly emphasized that one must be persistent and vigilant to defend your rights and to resist evil even in the civil arena (Luke 18:1-8). Passivity in the face of injustice was never condoned (Rom 12:21). Rather, He spoke of our calling to overcome evil with good and to work against poverty, slavery, and oppression (Luke 4:17,18). Christ emphasized the inherent value of every human, and therefore, the basis for equal rights and for government to serve the needs of the individual. Jesus also taught about limited government, jurisdictional boundaries, bringing social change gradually, and the validity of the civil laws of Moses and due process. (These principles are covered in detail in Chapter 6.) As the church propagated these principles throughout the pagan world, the Christian idea of man and government became clear. As Frothingham states:

> *"Christianity then appeared with its central doctrine, that man was created in the Divine image, and destined for immortality; pronouncing that, in the eye of God, all men are equal. This asserted for the individual an independent value. It occasioned the great inference, that man is superior to the State, which ought to be fashioned for his use;...that the state ought to exist for man; that justice, protection, and the common good, ought to be the aim of government."* [2]

The United States Declaration of Independence (1776) states these Christian ideas this way:

> *"We hold these Truths to be self-evident, that all Men are created equal, that they are endowed by their Creator with certain unalienable Rights, that among these are Life, Liberty, and the Pursuit of Happiness--That to secure these Rights, Governments are instituted by Men, deriving their just powers from the Consent of the Governed."*

Few nations today operate their governments based on the Christian idea of man and government, yet more and more are gradually rejecting pagan tendencies in government.

The Primitive Churches in the Roman Empire, 30-400 A.D.

As the early Church applied the personal and political principles that Jesus taught, they not only affected multitudes of lives, but also turned the entire known world upside down. Paganism was being overthrown throughout Europe as Christianity rapidly spread. By 500 A.D. about 25% of the world had become Christian and over 40% had been evangelized. [3]

In Chapter 6, we will look at some instances in the New Testament where the apostles resisted tyranny by various forms of civil protest and legal action (Acts 13, 16, 24, 25, 26). The second chapter of this book mentioned how the apostle Paul rebuked the Christians in Greece for their apathy and irresponsibility in regards to politics that allowed non-Christians to be in control (1 Corinthians 6:2-5). He urged them to seek public office such as in the local court system of Corinth. When the Christians found it difficult to make inroads in the Roman legal system, they began to form their own alternative courts, which were binding only upon those who voluntarily accepted the outcome by covenant agreement. Over time, the pagans began to reject the arbitrary Roman system and seek for real justice through the Christian courts. By the time of Constantine, around 300 A.D., half of the empire's population had been converted to Christianity and consequently were involved in the "Christian" court system. Thus, when Constantine made Christianity the official established religion of the empire, the Christian judges were also given legal status and, therefore, required to wear the official dark robe or gown worn by all civil magistrates. The modern practice of mainline denominational clergymen wearing "pulpit gowns" traces its origins to this act, because most of these "Christian judges" were clergymen. The "pulpit gown" therefore, is a testimony and memorial of the primitive churches being involved in politics.

Paul's exhortation to these Christians in Corinth was so strong that one of Paul's own staff -- a man named **Erastus** -- eventually switched from being a gospel minister to become a civil "minister" (Romans 13:4,6 - "Rulers are servants of God. . .a minister of God to you for good . ."). Erastus had been a full-time apostolic assistant to Paul, just like Timothy, until he was sent by Paul over to Greece (Acts 19:22). While ministering to the churches there, Erastus began to feel God's calling into political office. Paul tells us what happened to him when, in the close of his letter to the Romans (written from Corinth), Paul says: "Erastus, the city treasurer greets you" (Romans 16:23). Archaeologists have uncovered in Corinth a first-century tablet that reads: "Erastus, the Commissioner of Public Works, laid this pavement at his own expense." This is believed to be the Erastus of the Bible.[4]

What an exciting illustration of obedience to Christ's command to his disciples to be public **servants** once they gain positions in government! Here Erastus does something unprecedented in pagan Roman government -- he personally pays for the project instead of raising taxes -- and is honored with a special tablet. Here we have an example in the New Testament of Christians, not just protesting evil government, but taking the initiative to provide good government by seeking civil office -- and it is sanctioned by the greatest apostle of all!

Besides all this, the primitive churches provided a model of self-government with union among their congregations. Although church government on the local level was predominantly self-governing, there were certain limited powers in the hands of the apostles and elders of the churches at large who met in council at Jerusalem (Acts 15:2,4,6 and 16:4) and approved special ministries such as a poor fund which was administered out of Jerusalem (Galatians 2:1,2,9 and 2 Corinthians 8:19,23). The relationship between the mother church in Jerusalem and all the other new churches was the first example of federalism, or dual governments working both at once in defined spheres of jurisdiction (local and national). These churches were models of equality, service, monogamy, and compassionate use of private property for the needy. The principles of Christianity exemplified in these churches would gradually lead to the abolition of institutionalized injustices which were prevalent in every culture: polygamy, human sacrifice, oppression of women, slavery, racism, totalitarianism, and socialism.

However, as the centuries went on, the church gradually lost its virtue and Biblical knowledge and thus embraced elements of the pagan philosophy of government and education. This caused the clergy to think that only they could understand God's Word and, therefore, they must tell the common people what God required of them, instead of allowing every person to be self-governing and learn for themselves.

Instead of sowing the truth in the hearts of the people and allowing the inevitable fruit to grow, the clergy simply tried to externally dictate to the people what they thought God commanded (and what they thought was often quite contrary to the Bible).

The first pagan king to be converted was the king of Armenia in 295 A.D. He declared his nation to be "Christian" although it was not genuine. It was still a pagan form of monarchical government.

Constantine also attempted to accomplish God's will with pagan methods. After he was converted (about 312 A.D.) he desired to make his empire Christian. Yet not understanding God's method of gradualism, he superficially united the Church and State and set up a national church declaring all citizens in his empire must be Christians. His attempt at accomplishing that which was good hindered the work of God for centuries in an era which became known as the "Dark Ages," (beginning after the fall of the Roman Empire in 410 A.D.).

Celtic and Catholic Christianity in Europe, 400 - 1066

Christianity was introduced in Britain in the first century, possibly by Joseph of Arimathea. As the Celts were converted they established decentralized churches, unlike those that developed in the Roman and Byzantine Empires. This was mainly due to their being located on the outer edge of the Roman Empire where little power existed to control them.

By A.D. 150 the Pastors of the Celtic Churches preached in the common language from interlinear Bible translations called glosses. The greatest of the pastors was Patrick who left England and went to evangelize Ireland in the first part of the fifth century. King Loehaire was converted and made Patrick his counselor (termed "Anmchara"), in which capacity he worked to introduce Biblical Law into the civil realm. Patrick wrote *Liber Ex Lege Moisi* (*Book of the Law of Moses*) which was applied by local chieftains or kings throughout Ireland (as yet not a united political arrangement, only a Biblical/religious unity). It emphasized the rule of law and local self government. [5]

The Anglo-Saxons first came to Britain around 428 A.D. when two brothers, Hengist and Horsa, were invited to bring their relatives and help the king of Kent fight off his enemies. They stayed in Britain, and after some time eventually took the island over and named it Anglo-land, or Engel-land (today England).

Initially the Anglo-Saxons turned on the Celts, killing many of them. One time they killed 1200 Celtic Pastors in prayer. The Saxons may have conquered the Celts militarily, but the Celts conquered the Saxons spiritually. The Saxons were thus converted to Celtic Christianity. Roman Catholicism did not come to Britain until 597. After its introduction, the church in Britain, due to the Celtic influence, still emphasized the Bible above Papal authority.

Around 565 a follower of Patrick, named Columba, left Ireland and evangelized the king of the Picts (who lived in what is today Scotland). Columba also translated *Liber* in the Scottish language.

King Alfred

The first king who was revered enough to unite all of England into one nation was a Saxon known as **Alfred the Great,** who ruled from 871 to 899. Just before Alfred became king, most of England had been conquered by the Vikings from Denmark through a long series of fierce battles. Wessex, in the southwest portion of England, was the only region that remained for Alfred to rule. Almost immediately, and for years to follow, Alfred found himself in thick battle with the Danes. David Chilton writes of this struggle:

"In 876 the Danish chieftain Guthrum attacked Wessex in earnest with a powerful host, aiming to break Alfred's hold on the country once and for all. The Vikings succeeded: in the winter of early 878, Guthrum pushed Alfred into the marshes, where the king and a small group of loyal followers were forced to hide out on the Isle of Athelney. Historians have called this time of testing Alfred's "Valley Forge," where he had to bide his time while virtually all England was overrun with pagan enemies of the faith who sacked churches and monasteries, wiping out the tattered remains of a Christian past. The legends say, however, that the bold and daring Alfred entered the Viking camp disguised as a minstrel and actually performed for Guthrum and his chiefs -- getting a chance to listen to their plans and plotting his own strategy. When spring came, Alfred rallied the English army for a final push against the invader's vastly superior forces. This time Alfred was victorious. As the Anglo-Saxon Chronicle puts it, 'he fought against the entire host, and put it to flight.' The Vikings agreed never to attack Wessex again, and they submitted to the terms of peace.

"Alfred did not banish Guthrum and his men. He didn't have them executed, either. His solution to the problem of the Vikings seems incredible to us, but it worked. The peace treaty he imposed on them included this provision: that Guthrum and 'thirty of the most honorable men in the host' become Christians! Guthrum accepted the conditions, and he was baptized into the Christian faith, Alfred standing as his godfather. At the conclusion of the ceremony, Alfred embraced his newborn brother in Christ and threw a twelve-day feast for him and his men. And then, as if this weren't enough already, Alfred made the strangest political move of all. He said to Guthrum, in effect: 'My brother, this land is much too big for me to rule all by myself; and the important thing isn't who's in charge. The real issue is a Christian

England. So don't go back to Denmark. Stay here and rule this land with me, under the lordship of Jesus Christ.'

"*That's exactly what Guthrum did. In fact, when later groups of Danes tried to launch invasions against England, Guthrum and Alfred stood together as Christian kings, united in defense of a Christian land. As the first Viking leader to become a Christian, Guthrum foreshadowed the conversion of all the Norse peoples and their incorporation into the civilizations of Christendom.*" [6]

With the coming of peace, Alfred instituted Christian reforms in many areas including establishing a government that served the people. Alfred was taught how to read by a Celtic Christian scholar known as Asser, and studied Patrick's *Liber* and thus established the Ten Commandments as the basis of law and adopted many other patterns of government from the Hebrew Republic. The nation organized themselves into units of tens, fifties, hundreds and thousands and had an elected assembly known as the "Witen." These representatives were called respectively: a tithingman (over ten families), a vilman (over 50), a hundredman, and an earl. The earl's territory which he oversaw was called a "shire," and his assistant called the "shire-reef," where we get our word "Sheriff" today. The Witen also had an unelected House made up of the noblemen, but the king was elected; he was not a hereditary king. Their laws were established by their consent. Alfred's uniform code of Laws (890) was the origin of common law, trial by jury, and habeas corpus. Alfred's code was derived from Mosaic law and Jesus' golden rule.

Thomas Jefferson said that the Anglo-Saxon laws were "...the sources of the Common Law...[and] the wisest and most perfect ever yet devised by the wit of man, as it stood before the 8th century;..." The National Seal proposed by Jefferson in 1776 was to have on one side "the children of Israel in the wilderness, led by a cloud by day, and a pillar of fire by the night." On the other side Jefferson proposed images of "Hengist and Horsa, the Saxon chiefs... whose political principles and form of government we have assumed." [7] This is true because of the Saxons' contact with the Celtic Christians (British natives). The Saxon culture in Germany from which they originated provided no constitutionalism whatsoever.

Celtic Christians from Britain also went as missionaries to the continent and helped to shape its history. Some went to Czechoslovakia and Germany in the 5th century and sowed seeds, the fruit of which we will look at later. A Celtic-influenced British Christian named Alcuin, became the teacher and advisor to Charlemagne (Charles the Great) - the king of the Franks and the head of the Holy Roman Empire in 800 - and encouraged learning and the arts throughout Europe.

In eastern Europe, the Gospel started to impact such nations as Czechoslovakia (929 is the year of the martyrdom of prince Wencesles who embraced Western Christianity), Russia (987), and the Norse countries of Sweden, Norway and Denmark. One famous Norseman who became a Christian was Leif Erikson, the son of the Danish king Eric the Red. Leif was the first to discover America around 1000. In 1016 Iceland became a Christian nation.

The Bible and the Rebirth of Learning and Liberty, 1200-1500

Most nations were generally stagnant from 500 -1200 A.D. (except in Britain and some isolated regions). There was little or no advancement in civil liberty, scientific discoveries, technology, and most other areas. This lack of advancement was primarily a result of the light of the Word of God being "hidden" from the common people.

The Word of God was completed by the apostles in the first century and canonized in the following few centuries; yet as the church "backslid" from God, His Word was further removed from the people. Nevertheless, "the textbook of Liberty" was providentially being preserved by scribes and monks who painstakingly spent their entire lives hand-copying the Bible. The lack of access to the truth of the Bible kept the common people ignorant during the Dark Ages.

The middle east and northern Africa did see some advancement in learning and the arts during the middle ages, largely due to the impact of Mohammed on the Arab culture. The Islamic faith broke the power of polytheism and idolatry in the public arena of the middle east. Mohammed's civil successors were known as the Caliphate rulers and they encouraged learning and the arts in their Saracen culture (630-1200) which spread as far as France. They were unfortunately overcome by the more narrow-minded and violent Mongols and Turks who sparked the Crusades between 1100-1300 by attacking Christian pilgrims on their way to the Holy Land. The wisest and most upright of the Islamic Arab princes (i.e Sultans) was Saladin, who began to reign in 1192, but unfortunately for the future of the Middle East, was conquered by the Mongols led by Genghis Khan.

The Crusades were an unbiblical method employed to keep the Islamic faith from supplanting Christianity in the Middle East. In this the Crusades failed, yet they did keep Islamism from advancing deeply into Europe. In addition, Europeans who had participated in the Crusades and had seen the universities in the Middle East were inspired to start new schools in Europe. By 1170 universities sprang up in Bologna, Italy, Paris, France, and Oxford, England. This new hunger for learning, although still limited to small numbers of society, especially focused on the Bible.

In Italy, cities such as Venice, Pisa, Genoa, Ravenna and the leading city, Milan, declared independence and elected their own magistrates in 1054. The Emperor conquered these cities in 1162, but around 1100, Pope Gregory VII, in an effort to reduce the power of the Emperor, applied the teaching of a scholar from the Alsace-Lorraine area named Manegold (c. 1056) concerning the theory of **interposition,** meaning a lower magistrate has the right and duty to disobey and resist a higher authority if he acts contrary to the Law of God.

Around 1200, a Catholic monk named Dominique instituted the first example of representative government on a national level in England in his Order of Monks. This was in great contrast to most of Catholicism. This representative principle would be reflected in the civil realm when the English Parliament was created in 1262.

The Norman system of government, which began in England with William the Conqueror in 1066, removed the rights of the people. Consequently, the kings abused the people, barons as well as commoners. Things worsened to the point under King John that the English barons drew up a contract that addressed the abuses and guaranteed the barons certain rights and privileges as contained in Biblical law. King John, needing the help of the barons to raise money, reluctantly signed the Magna Charta in 1215. It is important to note that a Catholic clergyman, Stephen Langton, is likely the chief architect of the document. The Pope said it was illegal but the English Catholic Church, due to its Celtic origins, ignored the Pope and preserved the document and expounded it. The Magna Charta embodied the principle that both sovereign and people are beneath the law and subject to it. Later, both Englishmen and American colonists cited the Magna Charta as a source of their freedom.

In France, a Catholic scholar named Thomas Aquinas (1225-1274) and the Spanish Dominicans, disagreeing with the Franciscans, affirmed the inalienable right to property and the general doctrines of the law of nature and individual rights. This was almost 500 years before Locke wrote of the same ideas. In 1288, the first national assembly was convened in France by King Philip and confirmed his authority over the Pope's.

In 1308 in Switzerland, William Tell refused to render homage to the governor by not bowing to a hat that he had had placed on a pole in the city square. In consequence, Tell was sentenced to shoot an apple off his son's head. He succeeded but was arrested anyway. The injustice of the Austrian governor induced the Swiss Cantons of Uri, Schwitz, and Underwald to revolt from the Empire. Under the leadership of Milchtat, Staffacher, and Switz they succeeded, without shedding blood, in establishing the confederacy of Switzerland.

The spirit of liberty was spreading as a result of the spirit of free inquiry and learning that preceded it. Even the Emperor, Charles IV who lived in Prague, Czechoslovakia, was influenced by the spirit of the age. In 1355 he issued *The Golden Bull* which established a fixed number of seven electors with certain duties in the Empire. Charles also founded a university in Prague in 1348.

John Wycliffe in England (1382)

A Catholic clergyman who taught in the English university at Oxford, named John Wycliffe, began to see that "Scripture must become the common property of all" in order that there might be "a government of the people, by the people, and for the people." Up until this time only the educated, who were few, could read the Bible because it was only available in Latin or Greek and Hebrew. To accomplish a general reformation, he translated the whole Bible from Latin into English. This was completed around 1382, one hundred fifty years before the Protestant Reformation occurred.

He not only translated the Bible, but set out to implant the truth of the Scriptures in the hearts of all men. This was accomplished by distributing Bibles, books of the Bible, and tracts throughout all England.

His followers, called "Lollards" (a derogatory term meaning "idle babblers"), would travel to towns and villages passing out Bibles and tracts and preaching and teaching on street corners, in chapels, gardens, assembly halls, and everywhere else they had an opportunity. As most people were uneducated, the Lollards taught many how to read, including many nobles.

In the words of Prof. G. V. Lechler, the Lollards "were, above all, characterized by a striving after holiness, a zeal for the spread of scriptural truth, for the uprooting of prevalent error, and for Church reform. Even the common people among them were men who believed; and they communicated, as by a sacred contagion, their convictions to those around them. Thus they became mighty." The translation of the Bible in the hands of the Lollards became such a power, that at the close of the century, "according to the testimony of opponents, at least half the population had ranged themselves on the side of the Lollards." [8]

As prevalent error in the church began to be addressed, the church leaders showed their appreciation by trying to eradicate this *heretical* movement. Over the decades, they were able to stomp out most of the effects of Wycliffe's work and drive his followers underground, but the seeds of truth had been planted, that would later spring forth and produce a Reformation that no man could stop.

In 1425, hoping to remove all the traces of Wycliffe's *treachery*, the church ordered his bones exhumed and burned along with some 200 books he had written. His ashes were then cast into the little river Swift, "the little river conveyed Wycliffe's remains into the Avon, the Avon into the Severn, the Severn into the narrow seas, they to the main ocean. And thus the ashes of Wycliffe are the emblem of his doctrine, which now is dispersed all the world over." [9]

Jan Hus and Jerome in Czechoslovakia (1415)

Wycliffe's doctrine spread to Czechoslovakia primarily because Anna, the Queen of England who was Czech in origin, encouraged such thought there. She loved Wycliffe's teachings as did 30,000 other students who came to hear him from France, Germany, Holland and Switzerland. Many of the nobles and learned men who came with Anna from Czechoslovakia became his disciples and returned to their country with his books. One was professor Faulfash who taught in Prague University. He influenced Jerome and a minister named Jan Hus. Jan Hus was the Rector of the University and a preacher at the Chapel of Bethlehem in Prague. He taught the people the importance of Biblical Law and the conscience of the individual. Hus's often quoted sentence, that "it is better to obey God than the people," was sealed by his own death. Both Hus and Jerome ended up being burned at the stake for their beliefs by Emperor Sigismund, Jan Hus in 1415 and Jerome in 1416. The seeds of the Protestant Reformation of the 16th century were planted.

Liberating the Nations

Chapter 4

The Protestant Reformation in Europe

The Era of Invention and Discovery (1340-1516)

With John Wycliffe, the "Morning Star of the Reformation", the first rays of the light of God's Word began to shine forth in the darkness. His influence spurred a spirit of invention and discovery in the 15th century, the product of which assured that the light of the truth would never be put out by any civil or ecclesiastical government. One such event was the invention of the printing press by John Guttenberg around the year 1455. The first book printed by Guttenberg was appropriately, the Bible. Before this time, the only means of recording was by hand. It would take scribes over a year to hand copy one Bible. It's no wonder Bibles were scarce and expensive.

In the next century as the Reformation broke forth, the use of the printing press was instrumental in spreading the knowledge of liberty. Within 10 years of the invention of the press the total number of books increased from 50,000 to 10 million. Charles Coffin wrote:

"Through the energizing influence of the printing press, emperors, kings, and despots have seen their power gradually waning, and the people becoming their masters." [1]

Christopher Columbus

Another world-changing event was the voyage of Christopher Columbus to America. Columbus grew up in Genoa, Italy. The liberty in the northern Italian cities and the yearning for learning more about the east had sparked the travels of another Genoan, Marco Polo, around the year 1300. Polo's writings inspired Columbus who went to the Catholic monarchs of Spain and convinced them that it would be possible to reach the east by sailing west. In 1492, Christopher Columbus, whose first name meant "Christbearer", opened up the western hemisphere to Christian civilization.

We all know of this event, but do we know what motivated Columbus to embark on such an arduous and dangerous journey? The following excerpts from his *Book of Prophecies* will tell us:

> *"It was the Lord who put it into my mind -- I could feel His hand upon me -- the fact that it would be possible to sail from here to the Indies...*
>
> *"All who heard of my project rejected it with laughter, ridiculing me... There is no question that the inspiration was from the Holy Spirit, because He comforted me with rays of marvelous illumination from the Holy Scriptures... For the execution of the journey to the Indies, I did not make use of intelligence, mathematics, or maps. It is simply the fulfillment of what Isaiah had prophesied...*
>
> *"No one should fear to undertake a task in the name of our Savior, if it is just and if the intention is purely for His Service... The fact that the Gospel must still be preached to so many lands in such a short time -- this is what convinces me."* [2]

While Columbus discovered the New World, God did not allow the country from which he sailed to colonize the territory which originally comprised the United States. In 1478 the Roman Catholic Papacy began the Inquisition in Spain which wiped out virtually all protestants (as well as Jews and Moors) in that nation by 1558. The Protestant Reformation, therefore, never had a great influence in Spain's culture. This fact would have a detrimental effect on the development of the Spanish colonies in the new world. Columbus and other explorers, although motivated by sincere Christian devotion, carried with them the seeds of religious and civil tyranny. They transplanted the pagan ideas of government that still held sway in European minds at that time. God had plans for the United States to be planted with different seeds. Historian Daniel Dorchester writes:

"While thirst for gold, lust of power, and love of daring adventure served the Providential purpose of opening the New World to papal Europe, and Roman Catholic colonies were successfully planted in some portions, the territory originally comprised within the United States was mysteriously guarded and reserved for another -- a prepared people." [3]

In 1497, John Cabot, landing near the St. Lawrence River, laid claim to America for England. At this time, England, as all of Europe, lived under civil and religious tyranny, yet God would be at work in the sixteenth century to assure that this was changed.

American historian B.F. Morris writes of God's Providential hand at work during this era:

"No era in history is more signally and sublimely marked than that of the discovery and Christian colonization of the North American continent.

"The intervening century was in many respects the most important period of the world; certainly the most important in modern times. More marked and decided changes, affecting science, religion, and liberty, occurred in that period than had occurred in centuries before; and all these changes were just such as to determine the Christian character of this country. Meantime, God held this vast land in reserve, as the great field on which the experiment was to be made in favor of a civil and religious liberty. He suffered not the foot of Spaniard, or Portuguese, or Frenchman, or Englishman to come upon it until the changes had been wrought in Europe which would make it certain that it would always be a land of religious freedom." [4]

Martin Luther in Germany, 1482-1546

Martin Luther was God's instrument to awaken the conscience of man. His act of nailing his 95 theses on the church door at Wittenberg in 1517 is often referred to as a beginning point of the Protestant Reformation. Yet seeds of the Reformation had been planted many years before. About 100 years before, Jan Hus was burned at the stake for stressing Scripture authority instead of corrupt papal authority. He was directly influenced by Wycliffe's works. Hus influenced Luther by his example.

Luther's defense at the Diet of Worms in 1521 reveals that which characterized his life:

> *"I am... but a mere man, and not God; I shall therefore defend myself as Christ did, who said, 'If I have spoken evil, bear witness of the evil'...For this reason, by the mercy of God I conjure you, most serene Emperor, and you, most illustrious electors and princes, and all men of every degree, to prove from the writings of the prophets and apostles that I have erred. As soon as I am convinced of this, I will retract every error, and will be the first to lay hold of my books, and throw them into the fire...I cannot submit my faith either to the Pope or to the councils, because it is clear as the day that they have frequently erred and contradicted each other. Unless, therefore, I am convinced by the testimony of Scripture, or by clear reasoning, unless I am persuaded by means of the passages I have quoted, and unless my conscience is thus bound by the Word of God, I cannot and will not retract; for it is unsafe and injurious to act against one's own conscience. Here I stand, I can do no other: may God help me! Amen."* [5]

His life, and those of the reformers, can be summed up in the Latin phrase, *sola scriptura*, "Scripture alone." He translated the first German Bible in 1534. That was to be the basis of the reformers' thoughts and actions, rather than the decree of pope or king. It was Luther who brought forth out of darkness the great truth that we are justified by faith.

In 1540 Denmark, Norway, and Sweden became Lutheran nations.

John Calvin and Zwingli in Switzerland, 1509-1564

In 1534, when the French Protestant, John Calvin was 25, after having met with his cousin Robert Olivetan and Lefevre (the Bible translators), he left the Roman church in Noyon, France and was put in prison briefly. After his release, he lived in Paris for awhile in disguise and worshipped at secret meeting places in homes and in the woods by using passwords. But, later that year, he fled to Germany and then to Geneva, situated next to Lake Leman. This city had officially voted to be Protestant as a result of seeds planted by Ulrich Zwingli, the Zurich reformer, who was killed in battle in 1531 while serving as chaplain in the Swiss army. In 1536, Calvin wrote his famous *Institutes of Christian Religion.* In 1538, the Council of Geneva ordered Calvin to do something that he felt conscience bound to disobey. Then he was banished from Geneva and went to Strasbourg and pastored a French refugee congregation for three years where he also married a French refugee named Idelette. In 1541, Calvin was invited back to Geneva by the Council, and he wrote his *Ecclesiastical Ordinances,* which included policies for jails, education, and the physical health and safety of citizens, such as sanitation requirements.

The writings of John Calvin have probably had more impact upon the modern world than any other book, except the Bible. *"No writing of the Reformation era was more feared by Roman Catholics, more zealously fought against and more hostilely pursued, than Calvin's Institutes."* [6]

In his history of the Reformation, D'Aubigne writes:

> *"The renovation of the individual, of the church, and of the human race, is his theme...*

> *"The reformation of the sixteenth century restored to the human race what the middle ages had stolen from them; it delivered them from the traditions, laws, and despotism of the papacy; it put an end to the minority and tutelage in which Rome claimed to keep mankind forever; and by calling upon man to establish his faith not on the words of a priest, but on the infallible Word of God, and by announcing to every one free access to the Father through the new and saving way -- Christ Jesus, it proclaimed and brought about the hour of Christian manhood.*

> *"An explanation is, however, necessary. There are philosophers in our days who regard Christ as simply the apostle of political liberty. These men should learn that, if they desire liberty outwardly, they must first possess it inwardly...*

> *"There are, no doubt, many countries, especially among those which the sun of Christianity has not yet illumined, that are without civil liberty, and that groan under the arbitrary rule of powerful masters. But, in order to become free outwardly, man must first succeed in being free inwardly...*

> *"The liberty which the Truth brings is not for individuals only: it affects the whole of society. Calvin's work of renovation, in particular, which was doubtless first of all an internal work, was afterwards destined to exercise a great influence over nations."* [7]

Calvin worked hard to make Geneva a model of Biblical government. He established the first Protestant university in history known as the Geneva Academy whose rector was Theodore Beza. Geneva became a center of reform for not only Huguenot but also Protestant refugees from all over Europe. Puritan leaders of England, as well as John Knox of Scotland, studied under Calvin at Geneva.

The nation of the United States of America has been influenced greatly by Calvin, as D'Aubigne observed:

> *"Lastly, Calvin was the founder of the greatest of republics. The pilgrims who left their country in the reign of James I and, landing on the barren shores of New England, founded populous and mighty colonies, are his sons, his direct and legitimate sons; and that American nation which we have seen growing so rapidly boasts as its father the humble reformer on the shores of the Leman."* [8]

The Huguenots: The Protestants in France, 1523-1598

In 1523, just one year after Luther's New Testament translation into the German language and two years prior to Tyndale's English translation, Jacques Lefevre d'Etaples published the New Testament in French. The whole Bible was available in 1530 known as the *Antwerp Bible*. Another translation by Pierre Robert Olivetan was published in 1535. (It was revived in 1557 and became known as the Geneva Bible.)

Olivetan's cousin, John Calvin, fled persecution in France and settled in Geneva where he established a training center for many French Protestants. These Protestants became known as "Huguenots" which is a term from a German word meaning "confederates". Despite severe oppression, the Huguenots grew until in 1553 five were publicly burned at the stake. This event, instead of quenching the movement, fueled it, so that four years later one third of all Frenchmen were Protestants (about 300,000).

Two years later in Paris, a national synod convened and wrote the *Confession of Faith of the Reformed Churches* and the Pope responded by making the reading of the Bible illegal. Three years after this, in 1562, churches grew from 300 to 2000 throughout the land, and because of severe violations of their religious freedom they formed a political alliance to protect it. This plunged the nation into civil war between Protestant and Catholic powers. This conflict did not end until the *Edict of Toleration of 1598*, which guaranteed religious and political freedom in certain partitioned areas of the country.

In 1572, 30,000 Protestants were massacred while worshipping on St. Bartholomew's Day. The Huguenots became convinced of the necessity of using force in self-defense and articulated their Biblical reasoning of this in their *Vindiciae Contra Tyrannos (A Defense of Liberty Against Tyrants)* in 1579. This document, drafted by Philippe DuPlessis Mornay, drawing from reasoning found in Calvin's writings, became a precedent for the American Colonists at the time of their Revolution in 1776. An old Huguenot song said: "Spirit who made them live, awaken their children, so that they will know how to follow them."

Puritans and Separatists in England (1523-1588)

God not only prepares people to shape history, but He also shapes history to prepare people so that they may fulfill their destiny and accomplish God's purposes in the earth. This latter aspect of God's principle of preparation is evident in English history of the sixteenth century.

Henry VIII

Most people, when they hear of Henry VIII, think of his many wives. His first wife, Catherine of Aragon, had borne him no sons, plus he had acquired a particular fondness for Anne Boleyn, so he decided to divorce Catherine. Such action required permission from the pope, so Henry sent a petition asking for approval for the divorce. When he was denied approval, Henry, not being the submissive type, decided he would not only go on and divorce Catherine, but he would also divorce himself (and take England with him) from the Catholic Church.

Henry and England thus split from the Roman Catholic Church and around 1534 set up the Church of England in its place. At the time, the only difference in the two was that Henry was the pope over the Church of England instead of the Pope in Rome. However, this event would prove to be very important in the advancement of religious and civil liberty in England and throughout the world.

God was using Henry, who was not a godly man, to fulfill His purposes. Henry's actions to oppress any church reformers reveal that his split from Rome had nothing to do with godly reform, but only selfish desires; yet, God who governs in the affairs of men, was using this historical event to accomplish His will. While Henry broke from Roman Catholicism, there was still no freedom for individuals to worship God.

William Tyndale, 1494-1536

God's chief instrument in bringing about the Reformation in England was William Tyndale (1494-1536). Much of Tyndale's life was spent fulfilling his vision: *"If God preserves my life, I will cause a boy that driveth a plow to know more of the Scriptures than the pope."* [9] Tyndale's dream was accomplished, but only at a great cost.

He spent over twelve years in exile from his native country, all the time facing the possibility of being captured and put to death. During this time, he translated the Bible from the original languages with the idea of making it available for the common man. His New Testament was published in 1525. So scholarly was Tyndale's work that is has been estimated that our present English Bibles retain eighty percent of his original work in the Old Testament, and ninety percent in the New.

In 1536 Tyndale was betrayed, arrested, and killed as a heretic. On the day of his death, Tyndale calmly stated: *"I call God to record that I have never altered, against the voice of my conscience, one syllable of his Word. Nor would I this day, if all the pleasures, honors, and riches of the earth might be given to me."*

Before he was strangled and burned at the stake he prayed for King Henry VIII who had persecuted and put to death many reformers and caused Tyndale to flee his country. As he was being fastened to the stake he cried out with these final words: *"Lord, open the king of England's eyes!"* Although his life was extinguished, the flames of liberty would burn brighter than ever, for the Word of God would be spread to all people throughout England.

During Tyndale's life many copies of his New Testament were circulated throughout England, but only under cover for the king had banned Tyndale's work. Shortly after Tyndale's death, Henry VIII *"authorized the sale and the reading of the Bible throughout the kingdom,"* for he wanted *"to emancipate England from Romish domination,"* and saw the *"Holy Scriptures as the most powerful engine to destroy the papal system."* Ironically, the king put his approval on the Matthew Bible, which was in reality Tyndale's work under another name. In 1539 this Bible was revised and called the Great Bible, and was also promoted by Henry.

As the Word of God spread throughout the land, many people cried out with Tyndale, *"We know that this Word is from God, as we know that fire burns; not because anyone has told us, but because a Divine fire consumes our hearts."*

As we trace the hand of God in history and see various links in the Chain of Christianity, *"We should never forget that the prison, the scaffold, and the stake were stages in the march of civil and religious liberty which our forefathers had to travel in order that we might attain our present liberty."* [10]

The Puritan Movement Begins

When Henry VIII died in 1547, he left the throne in the hands of his son, Edward VI, and Edward's protectorates. They favored those who wanted further reform in the Church of England. Under Edward the Puritan movement was born. Those people desiring to purify the Church of its errors and ungodliness were called "purifiers" or "puritans".

These reformers were overjoyed when Edward assumed power, for they could now begin to freely carry out their desired reform. Yet, they learned that one righteous ruler is not enough to ensure reform within a nation.

Edward died in 1553, having reigned only six years. His half-sister and Henry's daughter, Mary, succeeded him to the throne. She has earned the title, *Bloody Mary*, for she put to death hundreds of reformers including the "first Puritan", John Hooper. It was Hooper who first denied the right of the State to interfere with religion in 1553.

Mary not only detested the church reforms that occurred under Edward, but also never liked the fact that her father had separated from the Catholic Church. She set about to make amends with the Pope and purge England of the Puritan movement. She caused 286 Reformed Anglican leaders, including Thomas Cranmer, Nicholas Ridley, and Hugh Latimer, to be burned at the stake.

Consequently, thousands of Puritans fled England to places in Europe that harbored reformers, and in particular, Geneva.

It was in Geneva that the English Puritans were taught much Biblical truth that they were lacking, in particular ideas on civil liberty. God made sure that the people He was preparing were equipped in every way. He even used Bloody Mary to help accomplish His purposes.

Elizabeth I and the Beginning of the Separatists

Mary died in 1558, after reigning only five years, and was succeeded by her half-sister, Elizabeth. This began the Elizabethan Era. Elizabeth did not want England to return to Catholicism, but she also was not interested in promoting the needed reforms within the Church of England. She did promise religious toleration which caused many Puritans to return to England who had fled during Mary's reign.

As the Puritans returned, they brought with them fuller ideas of civil and religious liberty, plus the Geneva Bible. While in exile in Geneva, a number of reformers translated and published a relatively compact and affordable Bible. The Geneva Bible would become the Bible of the masses. It was also the first English Bible to be divided into chapter and verse and included marginal notes which guided the people in a proper view of church and civil theology.

After a few years, Elizabeth saw her tolerance of reformers was causing many to cry out for more reform than she desired. So in 1562 she issued her *Articles of Religion* which prohibited further reform. At this, some of the Puritans gave up hope of ever seeing the needed church reform and separated themselves from the Church of England. Thus, the "Separatist" movement was born around 1580. The Pilgrims who first sailed to America in 1620 were English separatists.

The Separatist movement continued to grow throughout Elizabeth's long reign, although there were attempts from within England and from other nations to stop it.

The Miraculous Defeat of the Spanish Armada

In 1588, Philip II of Spain sent the Spanish Armada to bring England again under the domination of Rome. A historian of the period, Richard Hakluyt writes of this event:

"It is most apparent, that God miraculously preserved the English nation. For the L. Admiral wrote unto her Majestie that in all humane reason, and according to the judgement of all men (every circumstance being duly considered) the English men were not of any such force, whereby they might,

58

without a miracle dare once to approach within sight of the Spanish Fleet: insomuch that they freely ascribed all the honour of their victory unto God, who had confounded the enemy, and had brought his counsels to none effect.... While this wonderful and puissant Navie was sayling along the English coastes,... all people thorowout England prostrated themselves with humble prayers and supplications unto God: but especially the outlandish Churches (who had greatest cause to feare, and against whom by name the Spaniards had threatened most grievous torments) enjoyned to their people continuall fastings and supplications... knowing right well, that prayer was the onely refuge against all enemies, calamities, and necessities, and that it was the onely solace and reliefe for mankind, being visited with afflictions and misery..." [11]

Here is what happened: As the Spanish fleet sailed up the English Channel, they were met by the much smaller English navy. In the natural, the English had no hope, yet all of England had been fasting and praying. A storm arose which blew many of the Spanish ships up against the coast of Holland, causing them to sink. Oddly, the smaller English ships were not affected by the storm and were able to maneuver next to the Spanish ships and set many of them on fire. A few Spanish ships limped back to Spain without touching English soil.

God had providentially intervened to protect His people and ensure that England would fulfill its purpose as a nation. Even the nation of Holland acknowledged the hand of God. In commemoration of the event, they minted a coin. On one side were ships sinking; on the other, men on their knees in prayer with the inscription: *"Man Purposeth, God Disposeth,"* and the date "1588". [12]

William the Silent in Holland, 1579

The Catholic Monarch of Spain also tried to stamp out the Protestant Reformation in Holland, but was unable to due to the heroic leadership of Prince William the Silent and the Dutch people. The famous siege of Leyden in 1574 by the Spaniards failed when the Dutch people broke their dikes and flooded their own farms and homes in order to drive the enemy out.

"Better a drowned land than a lost land," they said. "We can pump it dry again, if we drown it, but if we yield to the Spaniards, our liberties are gone forever." [13]

After the Spanish King Philip put 100,000 "heretics" to death or threw them in jail, the people revolted and elected William as their leader. Philip offered the besieged town of Leyden a pardon if they would surrender but their only "crime" was that they had been reading the Bible and thinking for themselves. They would not accept a pardon for this.

The people answered: *"As long as there is a man left, we will fight for our liberty and our religion."*

Thousands began to die of starvation and the people began eating dogs, cats and rats to survive. A few faint-hearted ones urged the city's ruler to give up but Pieter Van der Werff replied: *"I have taken my oath to hold the city. May God give me strength to keep it! Here, take my sword; plunge it into my body; divide my flesh to appease your hunger, if you will; but, God helping me, I will never surrender!"*

The Spanish soldiers outside taunted the "rat-eaters", but the Leyden people shouted back: *"You call us rat-eaters. We are; but so long as you can hear a dog bark inside of the walls, you may know that the city holds out. We will eat our left arms, and fight with our right. When we can stand no longer, we will set fire to the city, and perish in the flames, rather than give up our liberties!"*

Then on the night of October 1, a wall of the city collapsed with a loud noise leaving the city wide open for the Spaniards to attack. However, the sound so frightened the Spaniards that they decided to retreat in the dark of night and thus Leyden was saved.

William and the people gave glory to God and Holland won their freedom and established a republic which became a refuge for persecuted Protestants. Leyden itself would become the home of the Pilgrims from England for 12 years before they moved to America in 1620.

John Knox and Samuel Rutherford in Scotland, 1559-1644

In 1433 a follower of Wycliffe named Paul Craw was martyred in Scotland. Other martyrs followed, including Patrick Hamilton (1528) and George Wishart (killed in the 1540's). The successor to Wishart in bringing reform to Scotland was John Knox. Knox fled to the European continent for a time and studied in Geneva under Calvin. While there, he helped develop the influential Geneva Bible and carried it with him when he returned to Scotland in 1559 to challenge Mary Queen of Scots. He brought reformation and established the Presbyterian system of church government in his country before he died in 1572. Although conquering Catholicism, the Reformers in Scotland eventually clashed with the Anglican Church and the people signed a national covenant in 1638 in Edinburgh to uphold their Presbyterian Faith. One of these Scottish Covenanters was a man named Samuel Rutherford who wrote *Lex Rex* or *The Law and the Prince* in 1644 to justify their defensive wars for their faith. He also was a representative in the Westminster Assembly which drafted their famous Confession of Faith.

The Suppression of Liberty in France and Czechoslovakia (1572-1618)

In 1572, France began to massacre its Protestants. 70,000 were killed while in worship on St. Bartholomew's Day which sparked a war that did not end until the *Edict of Toleration* in 1598. However, thousands of the French Protestants, known as "Huguenots," had already fled the country. The Reformation there never regained its former cultural force.

At first the martyrdom of Jan Hus and Jerome in Czechoslovakia backfired for the Emperor, because the Hussite resistance movement was birthed. The blind general Jan Zizka led the Hussites to miraculous victories in battle. In 1448, George, a Hussite, became King of Czechoslovakia with the motto: "God's Truth Prevails". Later, the Declaration of Kutna Hora in 1485 affirmed religious toleration in their nation, the first country in Europe to do so. The Czech Reformation birthed the Unity of Brethren Churches which flourished until the Thirty Years War began in 1618. The protestants in Czechoslovakia bore the brunt of the Catholic Emperor's wrath against Protestantism in Europe. The reform movement was completely suppressed there.

Thus both France and Czechoslovakia to this day have yet to enjoy the long-term gains that Protestantism purchased for most other countries in the rest of Europe. The lack of diversity and emphasis on the individual in France allowed such tyranny to prevail both in church and state that finally the French Revolution erupted in 1789 only to turn into the "Reign of Terror" and chaos that led once again to pagan monarchy under Napoleon. Only since 1989 have the Czech people finally overcome Communist centralized government.

In the next chapter we will see how these persecuted Christian groups migrated to America and established colonies based on their Christian ideas. Those nations' losses ended up being the world's gain for it made it possible for a nation made up of many races and nations, but having a common Biblical foundation, to rise up and become a model to the whole world.

Chapter 5

The United States and Liberty in Modern Times

Restoration of Biblical Church Government

There is a direct causal relationship between the dispersion of the Bible in the hands of the people and the rise of civil liberty. A survey of civil government from the time of Christ to the present reveals a sudden profusion of documents such as the Mayflower Compact, English Bill of Rights, and the Constitution beginning in 1620. Before this there existed only pagan monarchies.

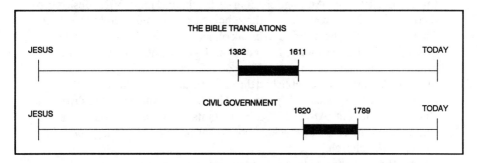

What produced these changes in ideas of government? How does one explain this? For two centuries prior to these changes, the Bible began to be translated and disseminated in the common language. It all began with

John Wycliffe in 1382 who said of his new translation into English: "This Bible is for the government of the people, by the people, and for the people."[1]

As people began to read the Bible, two things occurred: The church began to return to Biblical Christianity, and society began to be reformed and enjoy civil liberty. Christians in the religious system of the 16th century began to study the Scriptural model of church government.

The Original Corrupted and Restored

Three New Testament elements of church government were corrupted over time as the church backslid. Fewer and fewer believers were willing to love or lay down their lives and serve in the church. As this covenant commitment waned, most church functions were being performed by leaders rather than all members. Laziness and unspirituality among common believers led to a clear clergy-laity distinction by the third century.

As time progressed, even the elders became less exemplary and therefore fewer. Authority became more centralized in the hands of the most prominent and spiritual elders known as "bishops." In the body of Christ at large, this same apostasy led to fewer qualified apostles, and therefore more centralization of apostolic authority. Within a few centuries it was all centralized in the hands of the "Popes."

After many centuries the dispersion of the Bible produced a revival in Europe and a rejection of the papal centralization of power. Catholic Reformers known as "Protestants" sprang up within the Catholic church throughout Europe. An ungodly king of England, Henry VIII, desired to divorce his wife but could not without being excommunicated by the Pope. Therefore in 1534, he decided to break off from Rome and start the Church of England. The centralized form of church government, however, was the same, and became known as the Episcopal form.

In 1553 Protestants reestablished the role of elders in plurality (Presbytery) ruling the church instead of "popes." This became known as Presbyterian church government. Around 1570, Protestants known as "Separatists" began emphasizing the role of the whole congregation in participating and ministering in the church.

These three truths produced three distinct movements:

1. Episcopalians (1534) - emphasizing strong apostolic leadership.
2. Presbyterians (1558) - emphasizing plurality of elders.

3. Congregationalists (1570) - emphasizing covenant participation of all members.

The Movements Planted In the United States

Each of these movements settled in the American colonies in three major geographical areas. This was significant because their views of church government determined their colonial forms of civil government. Civil government is a reflection or a product of church government ideas. This relationship was clearly seen in the colonial civil governments.

The three religious movements settled in America in three geographical groupings: The Northern Colonies were settled predominately by Congregationalists, the Southern Colonies by Episcopalians, and the Middle Colonies by Presbyterians.

Each of these colonies established civil government that coincided with their view of church government:

1. Northern Colonies were self-governing (Democratic).
2. Middle Colonies were proprietary governments (which tended to be Aristocratic).
3. Southern Colonies were royal provinces ruled by a Governor (Monarchial).

Northern Colonies -- Bastion of Congregationalism

Massachusetts, 1620

At the English Queen Elizabeth's death in 1603, James I came to the throne. Intense persecution of Separatists under James' policies caused many of them to flee the country, this time to Holland. This was another Providential event that helped prepare those people who were to be "stepping stones" for the founding of a new nation -- one birthed by God.

From their earliest years in England through the establishment of the Plymouth Colony, the words and actions of the Pilgrims reveal their entire life was centered around God and doing his will. William Bradford, governor of Plymouth Colony for 33 years, relates how in their early years in Scrooby, England, these people's lives *"became enlightened by the Word of God, and had their ignorance and sins discovered unto them, and began by his grace to*

65

reform their lives..." But this enlightening brought much persecution from the religious system of England and after some years of enduring evil, the Pilgrims "*shook off this yoke of antichristian bondage, and...joined themselves (by a covenant of the Lord) into a church estate, in the fellowship of the Gospel, to walk in all his ways,...whatsoever it should cost them, the Lord assisting them.*"[2]

Their desire to worship God freely was costly, but God always assisted them. They first went into exile into Holland encountering troubles, poverty, and much hard work, but their Christian character enabled them to overcome the difficulties.

After 12 years in Holland they decided to sail to the new land of America. They desired a home where they could more freely worship God and that was more conducive to raising godly children than they had found in Holland. They were also motivated, in the words of Bradford, by *"a great hope and inward zeal...of laying some good foundation, or at least to make some way thereunto, for the propagating and advancing of the Gospel of the kingdom of Christ in those remote parts of the world; yea, though they should be but even as stepping stones unto others for the performing of so great a work."*[3]

When the Mayflower set sail on 1620, it bore more than just 102 Pilgrims and strangers, for the Pilgrims, more than any other single group, carried with them the culmination of all the world had known of religious and civil freedom. These principles based on the Christian religion were the seeds of a great nation.

After 66 days at sea the Mayflower reached America. The Pilgrims intended to settle just north of the Virginia Colony but were providentially blown off course and our from under the jurisdiction of the Virginia Land Company. Being unable to sail southward due to the weather they put ashore at Cape Cod. Had they arrived here some years earlier they would have been met by the Patuxet Indians and would have found no place to settle. These Indians had brutally murdered many white men who landed on their shores, but in 1617 a plague had mysteriously wiped them out and now neighboring tribes were afraid to come near the place for fear that some great supernatural spirit had destroyed them.

Being out from under the authority of the Virginia Company caused some of the non-separatists to talk mutinously of abusing their liberty once they went ashore, so before leaving the ship, the pilgrims drew up their own governmental compact which states:

> "...*having undertaken for the glory of God and advancement of the Christian faith, and the honor of our king and country, a voyage to plant the first colony in the northern parts of Virginia; do by these presence, covenant and combine ourselves together into a civil body politic...*" [4]

This document, the **Mayflower Compact,** placed the Pilgrim's civil government on a firm Christian base and was the beginning of American constitutional government.

In the Spring of 1630 some 1000 Puritans (which was more than the total inhabitants of the ten-year Plymouth Colony) sailed to America. They were led by John Winthrop, who served as the governor of Massachusetts Bay Colony for many years.

While at sea in passage to America, Winthrop wrote "*A Model of Christian Charity*" which contains their reasons for starting a new colony and the goals they wished to accomplish. Winthrop spoke of their desire to be "*as a city upon a hill*", where all the people of the earth could look upon and say of their own nation, "*the Lord make it like that of New England.*" [5]

In 1641, Massachusetts adopted the *Body of Liberties,* written by Rev. Nathaniel Ward, which was the first "bill of rights" in history.

Connecticut, 1636

In June 1636, Puritan minister Thomas Hooker and most of his Newtown congregation of about 100 people settled in what would become Connecticut Colony. Many others followed in the months to come. By May 1637, eight hundred people had settled in the valley. In January 1639 the *Fundamental Orders of Connecticut* were adopted as the Constitution of Connecticut. Rev. Hooker chiefly formulated this document, "*the first written constitution known to history.*" [6] This constitution, which contained many biblical rights and ideas expressed politically, would have a great influence on America. Historian John Fiske writes that the government of the United States is "*in lineal descent more nearly related to that of Connecticut than to any of the other thirteen colonies.*" [7]

Rhode Island, 1636

In 1636 Rev. Roger Williams purchased some land from the Indians and founded Providence, Rhode Island. In Williams' words, this was *"in a sense of God's merciful providence unto me in my distress"*.

His belief that the civil power has no jurisdiction over the conscience, was reflected in the laws of Providence and later in the colony of Rhode Island. Many others who had been persecuted for their religious convictions began settling in Rhode Island.

One excellent truth that Roger Williams helped to advance was that a free and prosperous civil state is dependent upon individuals and a church that are grounded in Biblical truth and at liberty to worship God. This is revealed in the Royal Charter of Rhode Island of 1663:

> *"The colonies are to pursue with peace and loyal minds their sober, serious, and religious intentions... in holy Christian faith;.... A most flourishing civil state may stand and best be maintained. .. with a full liberty in religious concernments... rightly grounded upon Gospel principles."*[8]

The Southern colonies -- Stronghold of Episcopalianism

Virginia, 1607

Jamestown was the first permanent English settlement in America. After the future settlers of Jamestown reached Virginia in April of 1607, one of the first acts of Captain John Smith and his soldiers was to erect a wooden cross on the shore at Cape Henry. It was at the foot of this cross that Reverend Robert Hunt led the 149 men of the Virginia company in public prayer, thanking God for their safe journey and recommitting themselves to God's plan and purpose for this New World. The Virginia Charter of 1606 reveals that part of their reason for coming to America was to propagate the *"Christian Religion to such People, as yet live in Darkness and miserable Ignorance of the true knowledge and worship of God."* One of the first converts to Christianity in America was the Indian princess Pocahontas. A painting of her baptism hangs in the rotunda of the United States Capitol.

The first representative assembly in America began in a church in James-town with the Rev. Bucke leading the elected government officials in prayer that God would guide and sanctify their proceedings to his own glory and the good of the plantation. They issued laws requiring church attendance, believing that men's affairs cannot prosper where God's service is neglected. In that same year, 1619, they also observed the first American Day of Thanksgiving.

North Carolina, 1653

Quakers and other religious dissenters from Virginia began to settle there in 1653 and nine years later obtained a Charter which acknowledged that the settlement was constituted for "...*the propagation of the gospel ... in the parts of America not yet cultivated and planted ...*" [9]

Georgia, 1731

Dr. Thomas Bray and General James Oglethorpe started the colony of Georgia in 1731 with about 100 settlers. The original settlers were followed in 1736 by Moravians and other persecuted Protestants who, when they touched shore, kneeled in thanks to God. They said, "*our end in leaving our native country is not to gain riches and honor, but singly this - to live wholly to the glory of God.*" The object of the devout Oglethorpe and others was "to make Georgia a religious colony" and so they laid out Savannah with numerous religious ceremonies and invited John and Charles Wesley and Rev. George Whitefield over to serve as chaplains, oversee Indian affairs, and build orphanages. When Whitefield died, the legislature attempted to have him buried there at public cost in honor of his influence.

The Middle Colonies -- Dominant Area of Presbyterianism (with Quaker and Catholic elements)

New York, 1628

This colony was originally started as two colonies in 1628 -- New Amsterdam and New Netherlands -- by Rev. Jonas Michaelius and others of the Dutch Reformed Church.

The first entry in New Amsterdam's city records (present day New York City) is Rev. John Megapolensis' prayer opening the court in 1653:

"Graciously incline our hearts, that we exercise the power which thou hast given us, to the general good of the community, and to the maintenance of the church, that we may be praised by them that do well, and a terror to evil-doers."

In 1665, the legislature passed an act to uphold "*...the public worship of God*" and instruction of "*...the people in the true religion.*"

Maryland, 1633

Maryland was started as a "reformed Catholic" colony, but became Protestant within a couple of decades. The governor, leading the expedition sent by Lord Baltimore, took possession of the country *"for our Lord Jesus Christ"* and made *"Christianity the established faith of the land."* One of the leaders wrote: *"bearing on our shoulders a huge cross, which we had hewn from a tree, we moved in procession to a spot selected ... and erected it as a trophy to Christ our Savior; then humbly kneeling, we recited with deep emotion the Litany of the Holy Cross."*

Father Andrew White wrote: *"Behold the lands are white for the harvest, prepared for receiving the seed of the Gospel into a fruitful bosom; ...who then can doubt that by one such glorious work as this, many thousands of souls will be brought to Christ?"*

In 1649, Maryland's Toleration Act stated that: *"...No persons professing to believe in Jesus Christ should be molested in respect of their religion, or in the free exercise thereof ..."*[10]

Delaware, 1638

New Sweden was established along the Delaware River in 1638 due to the backing of the heroic king Gustavus Adolphus who envisioned such a Protestant "planting" in the New World. It was settled by Rev. John Campanius and others of the Lutheran Church of Sweden.

Pennsylvania, 1681

Quaker William Penn was given the land between New York and Maryland in 1681. He said that *"my God that has given it to me...will, I believe, bless and make it the seed of a nation."*

In 1682 Penn wrote the colony's Frame of Government to establish "...*laws as shall best preserve true Christian and civil liberty in opposition to all unchristian licentious and unjust practices, whereby God may have his due, Caesar his due, and the people their due...*"
He states in the *Frame of Government of Pennsylvania:*

> *"Governments like clocks, go from the motion men give them; and as governments are made and moved by men, so by them they are ruined too. Wherefore governments rather depend upon men, than men upon governments...Let men be good, and the government cannot be bad; if it will be ill, they will cure it..."*

At a later time William Penn told the Russian Czar, Peter the Great, that *"if thou wouldst rule well, thou must rule for God, and to do that, thou must be ruled by him."* [11]

Biblical Reformation of Civil Government

In summary, the Christian religion was central in every colony in America. These early Americans saw that God desired to establish a nation where the church of Jesus Christ had the liberty to grow to maturity and be a light to the entire world.

There was Christian dominance in the settlement of every single colony. A joint statement made by all of the Northern Colonies in the *New England Confederation* of 1643 reflected the views of all 13 colonies. It stated: *"We all came into these parts of America with one and the same end and aim, namely, to advance the kingdom of our Lord Jesus Christ, and to enjoy the liberties of the Gospel in purity with peace."*[12]

Each of the original colonies, when examined to see the type of people and ideas that comprised the seed of the American Christian republic, reveal to us a unifying foundation of Christianity, although with that unity there existed great diversity. Each colony developed its form of government until the Revolutionary period when they were blended together under the national Constitution. Elements of *all three* forms of government are seen in America today:

1. Episcopalian or Monarchial elements found in the President and Governors.

2. Presbyterian or Aristocratic elements found in the Judges and originally in the U.S. Senators.

3. Congregational or Democratic elements found in the U.S. and State Representatives.

Even as none of the forms of church government alone constitutes the Biblical model, so also the Christian form of civil government must be a composite of all three. Episcopalian, Presbyterian and Congregational forms *together* make Biblical Church government. Monarchy, Aristocracy and Democracy *together* make a Biblical civil Republic. This indeed was what God providentially arranged in the establishment of the United States of America.

The American Christian Revolution and Constitution

The American Revolution was a Christian Revolution, not simply because it was led by great Christian men such as Samuel Adams, but because of the Biblical worldview which united the Colonies and motivated their actions and means of resistance. Thomas Jefferson wrote the *Declaration of Independence* based on Christian ideas of resistance and liberty. The Continental Congress repeatedly sought God in prayer and acknowledged Him in their proclamations and Legislation. Patrick Henry urged the use of arms as a biblical third step in resistance. George Washington led the American armies urging prayer among his troops and doing so himself frequently. Washington relinquished his power as commander of the armies and promoted the drafting of a new Constitution and became the first President by godly means rather than by a coup.

The *Declaration of Independence* is based upon the Christian idea of man and government. In fact, it was the first national covenant in history with such a foundation. The Declaration ends with the Congressional Representatives *"appealing to the Supreme Judge of the World"* and acknowledging *"a firm reliance on the protection of Divine Providence."*

After the signing of the *Declaration of Independence*, Samuel Adams, the father of the American Revolution, stated: *"We have this day restored the Sovereign, to Whom alone men ought to be obedient. He reigns in heaven and...from the rising to the setting sun, may his kingdom come."*[13]

72

America's founders understood that the birth of their nation marked the birth of the first Christian nation in history -- Christian not because all who founded it were Christians, but because its system of government was founded thoroughly upon Christian principles. J. Wingate Thorton relates how the sixth U.S. President, John Quincy Adams, said that, *"The highest glory of the American revolution was this: it connected in one indissoluble bond, the principles of civil government with the principles of Christianity."*[14]

The U.S. Supreme Court has concurred with this a number of times. For example, in 1892, it declared:

"Our laws and our institution must necessarily be based upon and embody the teachings of the Redeemer of mankind. It is impossible that it would be otherwise; and in this sense and to this extent our civilization and our institution are emphatically Christian... this is a Christian nation."[15]

The chief author of the American Constitution, and justly called its "Father," was a Christian statesman, James Madison. (He would also become the 4th U.S President.) That the Constitution was the product of Christianity and its ideas of man and government is revealed by the Biblical functions of government Madison listed in its preamble:

1. To establish justice - This is the goal of the passages in Romans 13 and 1 Pet 2:14 which say that government is to punish evildoers and protect those who do right.

2. To insure domestic tranquility - This phrase comes from the focus of prayer for government which Paul urged in 1 Tim 2:1,2. The New American Standard Bible says to pray for government "in order that we may lead a tranquil and quiet life in all godliness and dignity".

3. To provide for the common defense - The protection of innocent human life is at the base of not only capital punishment (Gen 9:6) but also in the provision of an army for protection from external threats.

4. To promote the general welfare - Romans 13:4 says that civil rulers are servants "to you for good". The common good of all classes of citizens must be promoted by government passage of laws guaranteeing equal opportunity. It is not proper for government to provide money and aid to special interest groups. It is to promote, not provide, and to do so for all people in general, not for special people.

5. To secure the blessings of liberty - Blessings are a gift of one's Creator, not a privilege granted by government. These blessings include life, liberty and property. A Biblical view of government sees that it cannot provide these, only secure them.

Besides all these goals which are Biblical, the United States Constitution established all of the basic structures that a Biblical framework of government should have. These will be discussed more fully in Chapter 11, *The Framework of Godly Government*. Although not perfect, the U.S. Constitution clearly represents the fullest expression of Biblical ideas and structures of government. For this reason it has lasted for over 200 years and has been copied by many nations around the globe.

The Development of the Chain of Liberty in the 19th and 20th Centuries

In the last two hundred years, the Chain of Liberty has spread and strengthened especially in Latin America and Africa and Australia. In South America Simon Bolivar led independence movements in numerous countries against Spanish control and helped to establish constitutions modeled after the United States. However, the fruit of these nations were much different than in the U.S. due to a lack of the fundamental principles in the lives of the people, which is necessary to support free, just, and prosperous nations (see Chapter 1). This lack of principles was due to a lack of access to the Bible. U.S. President James Monroe supported these revolutions with the announcement of his famous Monroe Doctrine in 1823.

European countries also began to throw off their oppressors and establish constitutional government. Some revolutions, as with that in France in 1789, unfortunately, were not founded solidly on Biblical methods of social change or on a Biblical philosophy of government and, therefore, reverted to pagan centralization after a period of chaos.

In England and the United States, further reform toward a fully Christian idea of man came about with the abolition of slavery (1833-1865), although it would take a Civil War in the United States to accomplish this due to Americans gradually falling away from God. There was also apostasy from Biblical ideas of civil life in America in the area of education -- the responsibility was turned over to government and the Bible was replaced with evolutionary dogma and secular humanism. Both the Europeans and the Americans adopted paganistic ideas of government and welfare. In foreign affairs, the United States begin to act in an unprincipled manner in many situations. The United States did, however, lead the way in dealing with racism and promoting the cause of civil rights and human rights. This has helped bring reform in many nations.

The march of the Gospel worldwide has increased overall at a rapid pace in the past two centuries. A rapid growth of Christians has occurred in the nonwhite countries in recent decades. Africa has seen a 2300% increase in the number of Christians on that continent since 1900. At least 35% of Africa is Christian (some estimate as high as 50%). In Asia the number of Christians has increased 1100% since 1900. While only 7% of Asia is Christian today, we can expect that figure to dramatically increase in the future.

While there has been a great growth in the numbers of Christians in many countries, there has been a slow change in the social and civil structures of many of these places. Why is this? Look, for example, at the situation in Africa. From 1900 to the present, the percentage of the Christian population has risen from 1% to 35% (perhaps 50%). Yet, in 1988 over 80% of Africa was controlled by communist/marxist or dictatorship/military rule. If historically the gospel liberates, what has been happening here?

Some advancement has occurred in instilling freedom, justice, and prosperity, yet it has been quite slow due to the lack of preparation in the heart and mind of the people -- they have not been prepared to support liberty. The home and the church are the primary institutions of such equipping, but they themselves have not been prepared in Biblical character **and** a Biblical world-view because the missionaries and church leaders who participated in the great growth of the Christian community embraced the heresy of dualism which considers only religious activity as spiritual and all other spheres of life as worldly. This heresy has been strengthened by unbiblical concepts of strict separation of church and state, which has kept Christians out of politics and public affairs.

As more Christians have begun to reject this false doctrine and have become salt and light in all aspects of life, we have seen, and will continue to see, the spread of liberty throughout the world.

Liberating the Nations

Chapter 6

Christ's Teachings On Public Affairs

Christ's Purpose: Internal and External Liberty

Why did Jesus come into the world? There are many answers to this question. He came to seek and to save those who are lost, He came to destroy the works of the devil, and He came to establish the Kingdom of God, to name a few. We have seen how man lost his ability to be self-governed when he disobeyed God. This led to external governmental tyranny. Christ also came to restore to man the potential of being self-governing under God. As mankind begins to be self-governed, it will have an effect on the external government's operating on his life. Jesus came to not only bring internal salvation, but also external political freedom.

After Jesus had risen from the dead and before He ascended into heaven, He gathered His disciples together. Acts 1:6-8 states:

> "And so when they had come together, they were asking Him saying, 'Lord, is it at this time You are restoring the kingdom to Israel?' He said to them, 'It is not for you to know times or epochs which the Father has fixed by His own authority; but you shall receive power when the Holy Spirit has come upon you; and you shall be My witnesses both in Jerusalem, and in all Judea and Samaria, and even to the remotest part of the earth.'" (Acts 1:6-8).

Of what type of kingdom were Jesus' disciples speaking? They were speaking of an external civil kingdom. For centuries the Hebrew people had

77

read the prophecies of Scripture declaring a Messiah would come and set up His throne and deliver the people from bondage. While Jesus walked on the earth, many of His followers thought He would set up His reign at any time. They even tried to make Him King. His disciples did not understand how His Kingdom was going to come.

While they had not seen it established during Jesus' ministry on earth, surely now that He had risen from the dead, He would restore the Kingdom. That's why they asked Him this question.

Jesus did not deny that an external expression of the Kingdom would come. In fact, He said that times and epochs would follow (which we can look back upon today) that would contribute to the establishment of the Kingdom and the extension of external and internal liberty "to the remotest part of the earth."

The "power" for this external establishment of liberty is the "Spirit of the Lord"; therefore, Jesus emphasized the receiving of this "power" through the receiving of the Holy Spirit. He knew the inevitable result of internal liberty would be external liberty.

Seven Political Principles that Jesus Taught

Jesus did not specifically lay out external plans for setting up a godly civil government. He more importantly dealt with the "spirit" or "power" by giving certain principles, and knew that a godly "form" would follow. Knowing that internal liberty would move outward, Jesus provided some principles and guidelines on civil government. These include:

1. Gradual Democratic Change - Internal to the External

God's pathway to liberty is from the internal to the external. While God desires us to work to establish an external expression of His Kingdom on earth (Matt 6:10 "Your Kingdom come, Your will be done on earth as it is in heaven"), this kingdom must first begin in the heart of man, and then it will naturally express itself externally in all aspects of society. The Bible reveals that "where the Spirit of the Lord is, there is liberty" (2 Corinthians 3:17). When the Spirit of the Lord comes into the heart of a man, that man is liberated. Likewise, when the Spirit of the Lord comes into a nation, that nation is liberated. The degree to which the Spirit of the Lord is infused into

78

a society (through its people, laws, and institutions), is the degree to which that society will experience liberty in every realm (civil, religious, economic, etc). Christ came to set us free (Gal. 5:1,3). Spiritual freedom or liberty ultimately produces political freedom. External political slavery reflects internal spiritual bondage.

Matthew 12:18-21 states that Jesus came to "declare justice to the Gentiles" and "establish justice in the earth" (Isa 42:1-4), and that He does it in a gentle manner. "He will not quarrel nor cry out, nor will anyone hear His voice in the streets" as He helps overcome evil with good. Although Jesus intends to "liberate the oppressed" and to help those in slavery and poverty (Luke 4:17,18), His basic method of change is the same for nations as it is for individuals -- we are gradually transformed as we apply the truth of His word to our lives. Dr. Augustus Neander reveals in his 1871 book, *General History of the Christian Religion*, how Christianity has historically brought about change in various nations of the world. Neander writes:

> *"Again, Christianity, from its nature, must pronounce sentence of condemnation against all ungodliness, but at the same time appropriate to itself all purely human relations and arrangements, consecrating and ennobling, instead of annihilating them...That religion which aimed nowhere to produce violent and convulsive changes from without, but led to reforms by beginning in the first place within, --whose peculiar character it was to operate positively rather than negatively, --to displace and destroy no faster than it substituted something better..."* [1]

Christian reforms within a nation do not begin with external or violent means (quite a contrast to Marxist/Communist "reforms" we see today), but they begin within.

In dealing with unbiblical situations in the nations today, we must remember that reform begins within, and as we remove that which is culturally detrimental we must simultaneously substitute something positive. A government-controlled and funded welfare system is unbiblical, yet the solution is not to pass a law that immediately eliminates civil government support of the needy. Individuals and churches must begin to fulfill their God-given responsibility in this area (substitute the good) as we work to remove the role of our civil government.

Neander goes on to say:

79

"Yet Christianity nowhere began with outward revolutions and changes, which, in all cases where they have not been prepared from within, and are not based upon conviction, fail of their salutary ends. The new creation to which Christianity gave birth, was in all respects an inward one, from which the outward effects gradually and therefore more surely and healthfully, unfolded themselves to their full extent." [2]

External liberty, then, must come gradually, not immediately. It was this mindset of immediate civil change that Christ sought to change in His parable found in Luke 19:11-17. The "nobleman" in the parable, who is a type of Christ, emphasizes to his servants that their responsibility is to "occupy" or "do business" with their earthly finances, time and talents until He returned. The reward for the faithful was that they would be given "authority over cities."

In other words, Jesus was giving a clue to Christians as to how to positively obtain influence and authority in civil government. It is not to be imposing Biblical Law upon people, but by consistent hard work and service to meet the needs of society around us, that we convince even non-Christians of the validity and excellence of Biblical ideas and solutions. It comes about through democratic process, not by coercion. Legislation that is in conformity to Biblical Law is possible only to the extent that Christians have been a part of their culture and "occupy" until He comes.

Through Christ, God releases the "Law of Liberty" into society through the cleansed hearts of men (James 1:25 & 2:12). This does not mean that the Old Testament law is done away with, but that man can now carry out the law, for God has empowered us to do so. The more a nation applies His law, the more that nation will prosper and walk in liberty. The degree which a people apply the law personally will be reflected through their governmental institutions, for the law flows from the heart of man out to the nation. The church disciples nations (Matt 28:19) by discipling and teaching people to contribute positively in the democratic process of change from the bottom up, not the top down -- from the internal to the external.

2. Civil Government is a Divinely Ordained Institution

In answer to Pilate, Jesus said, *"You would have no authority over Me, unless it had been given you from above"* (John. 19:11). Here Jesus asserts that civil authority is delegated and controlled by God. Paul states this in Romans

13:1 by saying, *". . . there is no authority except from God, and those which exist are established by God."* This also means that God is sovereign in human history and government; He is "the ruler over the kings of the earth" (Rev 1:5). This idea is important because the typical Christian today tends to view civil government as something "worldly" and unspiritual and, therefore, it is not necessary for the believer to study about or be involved in government. Spirituality involves more than religious and ecclesiastical topics.

3. Limited Government / Jurisdictional Boundaries

While God cannot be separated from government, since He ordained it, Jesus does speak of limits of jurisdiction of the state. The jurisdiction of the family and the church are also limited and defined in the Bible. Jesus taught that we are to render *"to Caesar [the state] the things that are Caesar's, and to God the things that are God's"* (Matt.22:17-21). Government does have certain legitimate rights to which we should give our allegiance, but they are very limited. One thing that belongs to the state and not the individual or any other institution is the use of the sword to protect the citizenry (Rom. 13:1-4). This means that we are to serve in the military if asked to do so (1 Sam 8:11-17). [God did allow nonparticipation by those whose conscience was violated.]

Another legitimate function of the state that Jesus clearly affirms in Matthew 22 is the collection of taxes (see also Matt. 17:24-27; Rom. 13:6-8). "Rendering to Caesar" (government) in a representative republic would also mean that we are to serve on juries, be involved in the political parties, and vote. Some things that belong to God and not the state include our worship of God (religion), our children and their education (schools), our property (free market), and our ideas (free speech and press). In these matters, the state has no authority and should not interfere or attempt to control. The church, the market, the press, and the schools are to remain completely free and independent.

4. The Inherent Value of the Individual

When Jesus referred to the image of Caesar on the money in Matthew 22, He, by implication and contrast, said that anything having the image of God on it is not under Caesar's jurisdiction. We are stamped with the image of

God since we were created by Him. The value of individual life is taught throughout scripture.

The sanctity of human life was the foundation for the establishment of government beginning with Noah (Gen 9:6). Because man is made in the image of God, Jesus taught that each person has worth regardless of what they can do. This contradicted the pagan idea that an individual was regarded as valuable only if he could contribute something to the state, or if he belonged to a certain social class or race. The individual is superior to the state or any collective interest. This is the principle of individuality. Clearly, Jesus and the primitive Christians exhibited the value that God places on all human beings regardless of race, class, handicap or gender (John 3:16).

5. Government is to serve all men equally

The inherent value of the individual and his superiority to the interests of the state, leads directly to another principle which we can read of in Luke 22:25-26. This is clearly a teaching about government and politics. Jesus said that: *"The kings of the Gentiles exercise lordship over them, and those who exercise authority over them are called 'benefactors.' But not so among you; on the contrary, he who is greatest among you, let him be as the younger, and he who governs as he who serves"* (NKJV) *(see also Mt. 20:25-26).*

Jesus is making reference to civil authorities, and is declaring that they are to be public servants. Therefore, the purpose of civil government is to serve people. This was a radical, new idea, and it contrasted greatly with the pagan idea of rulers dominating the people, an idea which existed throughout the entire world at this time. This declaration of Caesar not being the lord over the people was later to become evidence for charges of treason brought against Christ. As we will see, this idea gradually leavened many nations of the world, especially the United States. Today America calls her civil leaders "public servants." Many nations call their main leader the "Prime Minister" or in other words their "chief servant"! This world-changing concept goes straight back to Jesus Christ who, according to many Christians, had nothing to say about government! That the civil government is the servant of man is a Christian idea.

Not only is government to serve man, but it is to serve all men **equally.** All men are created equally in the image of God. This is not to mean that all men are born with the same physical abilities or talents or the same intelligence or property. These are external things which vary. But all men (and women) are born with the same internal rights: the right to live, worship, speak, think, work, and travel according to how he sees fit. Marxism and socialism tries to guarantee every man the equality of externals, but God's word simply states that every individual regardless of race, class, gender, or handicap should be protected by government in his opportunity to exercise his internal rights.

Jesus and the early church condemned discrimination and prejudice and partiality in treatment (James 2; 3:9; Acts 15:2-11; Gal. 3:28).

6. The Civil Laws of Moses/Fundamental Rights

Jesus clearly affirmed that the Laws of Moses were to be maintained in the culture unless specifically modified by the New Testament (Matt 5:17-19). He did not abolish any of the moral laws; only the ceremonial laws that were fulfilled by His sacrifice for sin were rendered obsolete. Jesus affirmed the laws against murder, adultery, dishonoring of parents, theft, and perjury. (Matt 5:21,27; 19:18-19; Matt. 15:4). He also affirmed the laws concerning divorce (Matt 5:31; 19:7-9), concerning oaths (Matt 5:33), and concerning equitable punishment and restitution (Matt 5:38). Jesus clearly affirmed the right to private property, and a free market for exchange and making a profit when accompanied by compassionate use of wealth for the poor and needy (Matt. 25:14-30; Luke 19:11-27; 16:11). This is "Christian" capitalism.

The Law of Moses against adultery requiring the death penalty was not abolished by Christ in the situation when the woman was brought to him caught in adultery (John 8:1-7). The only thing Jesus said was that the legal process must be followed properly using impartial juries and at least two witnesses in order to prove guilt - thus upholding the principle of due process and the right of appeal in the Law of Moses (John 8:7; Deut 17:4-7; 19:15; Matt 18:16). This formed the basis of our modern legal system that protects those charged with crimes until proven guilty by a fair trial.

It should also be noted that Jesus taught that one should avoid litigation as much as possible (Luke 12:58).

7. Using Political Means to Achieve Social Justice

Jesus also taught that there is a time when one should get involved in the legal and political system in order to defend one's rights and to address injustice. Luke 18:2-5 primarily teaches us about persistence in prayer, yet is based on a civil setting for achieving justice which Christ clearly affirms (Lk. 18:6-8). It is not unbiblical to pursue social change through governmental systems. We will look more at the methods Christians can use to bring about social reform at the end of this book.

Now we will focus on the Biblical methods for addressing injustice when a government ruler acts in a tyrannical manner. There may come a time when we must resist unlawful authority, i.e. a tyrant. If so, we must be prepared to suffer the consequences of resisting. To best achieve the desired results we must also recognize that there are steps we should take in our resistance:

Christ's Guidelines for Addressing Injustice

1. Protest or Legal Action

Our first means of recourse should be to protest and/or to take all legal action possible. Jesus instructed His disciples to publicly protest if city officials denied them their inalienable right to religious speech. He told them to go out into the streets and say, "Even the dust of your city which clings to our feet, we wipe off in protest against you" (Luke 10:11). "Wiping off the dust" is equivalent to boycotting. The free nations of the world generally have more means of legal recourse and of protesting ungodly action than do others. Examples of protesting include picketing abortion chambers, boycotting stores that sell pornography, and removing our children from public schools that deny God. We who live in free nations not only have the right to do this but are obligated to God to do so to keep our consciences clean.

Protesting unlawful action is a Christian idea. "Protestants" originally received this title due to their protesting against activities and authorities (civil and ecclesiastical) which were ungodly. In Acts 16 we read how Paul and Silas were unlawfully thrown into jail. When the chief magistrates tried to cover this up, Paul, recognizing his civil liberties were a sacred cause, demanded restitution to be made.

> *"Paul said to them, 'They have beaten us in public without trial, men who are Romans, and have thrown us into prison; and now are they sending us away secretly? No indeed! But let them come themselves and bring us out.'" (Acts 16:37).*

The chief magistrates did come and bring them out themselves.

Even when non-Christians apply Biblical methods for resisting tyranny they find some measure of success. An example is Gandhi in India.

There are six Biblical ways to protest:

1. Private appeals

(1 Sam. 19:1-5; Esther 3:11-14; 4:13-16; 7:5,6,10; 1 Kg. 12:1-15)

2. Non-cooperation, boycotting

Jesus protested when He remained silent before Pilate and refused to cooperate (Mt 27:14). When Paul and Barnabas were driven out of Antioch by the city officials, *"they shook off the dust of their feet in protest against them"* (Acts 13:51) as Jesus had instructed them (Lk. 10:10-11).

3. Litigation

(Luke 12:58; 18:1-5; Acts 21-26) The reason Paul appealed to Caesar within the Roman court system in Acts 24-26 was because his civil rights had been violated. He was being a good steward of the civil liberties God gave to him. The whole course of Paul's life was changed due to his exerting his rights as a citizen. He saw this action as part of the Great Commission.

4. Public visible rallies, marches, demonstrations

(Luke 10:10,11; Isa. 20, Jer. 13; Ezek 3,4,24,33; 1 Kg. 18:19-21; Matt. 3:1-4) Jesus publicly censured Herod for his death threats (Luke 13:31-32).

5. Blocking access; non-violent intervention

(Mark 11:15,16)

6. Disobeying unjust laws

(Acts 5:29; 4:19,20; Dan 6:10; 2:49; 3:4,5,16-18; Exod 1:15-17; 2:2,3; Esther 4:10-16; 3:1-4,6-11; Ezra 4:17,21-24; 5:1-3; Haggai 2:1,2,4-9; 1:12-14).

2. Flight/emigration

If all avenues of protest or legal action are expended to correct unlawful acts of civil authorities, then flight, if possible, is the next appropriate measure to take. Jesus told His disciples that "whenever they persecute you in this city, flee to the next" (Mt. 10:17,18,23). He also warned them to flee the destruction that was to come upon Jerusalem (Mt. 24:15-18). Seeking a safe refuge/sanctuary for hiding can be considered a form of flight. The early church took flight as persecution rose against them (Acts 8:1-4). Sometimes flight to other places will more surely allow us to fulfill God's will.

Many people who came to settle in America were fleeing civil and religious tyranny. After exhausting all means of protest and legal action, they saw that flight was the best means of accomplishing God's purpose. This principle is the basis of the Constitutional right of emigration.

3. Force in self-defense

As a last recourse in resisting tyranny, force is a legitimate biblical means. The Old Testament contains many examples of God's people using force to defend themselves. We will examine in a later lesson how a defensive war in a just cause is sinless, but for now we want to show that Jesus personally affirmed the legitimate use of force at certain times in resisting tyranny.

At the conclusion of the Last Supper, Jesus continued His instructions to the seventy disciples that He had begun earlier (Luke 10) by instructing them to arm themselves militarily:

> " 'Let him who has no sword sell his robe and buy one.' And they said, 'Lord, look, here are two swords.' And He said to them, 'It is enough.' " (Luke 22:36-50) (see also Matthew 26:50-56)

Here, Jesus confirms the legitimacy of using force at certain times.

John Jay, the first Supreme Court Justice of the United States and author of the Federalist Papers, commented on this incident in a letter written in 1818:

> "Although just war is not forbidden by the gospel in express terms, yet you think an implied prohibition of all war, without exception, is deducible from the answer of our Lord to Pilate, viz: 'If my kingdom were of this world, then would my servants fight, etc.'"

> "At the conclusion of the Last Supper, our Lord said to his disciples: 'He that hath no sword, let him now sell his garment and buy one.' They answered: 'Lord, here are two swords.' He replied: 'It is enough.'"

> "It is not to be presumed that our Lord would have ordered swords to be provided, but for some purpose for which a sword was requisite."

> "When the officers and their band arrived, with swords and with staves, to take Jesus, they who were about him saw what would follow. 'They said unto him: Lord, shall we smite with the sword?'" (Luke 22:49). It does not appear that any of the eleven disciples were with him, except one, made the least attempt to defend him. But, Peter, probably inferring from the other swords, that they were now to be used, proceeded to 'smite a servant of the high-priest,

and cut off his right ear' (vs. 50). Jesus (perhaps, among other reasons, to abate inducements to prosecute Peter for that violent attack) healed the ear."
"He ordered Peter to put his sword into its sheath, and gave two reasons for it. The first related to himself, and amounted to this, that he would make no opposition, saying: 'The cup which my Father hath given me, shall I not drink?' The second related to Peter, viz., they who take the sword, shall perish by the sword (Matt 26:52); doubtless meaning that they who take and use a sword, as Peter had just done, without lawful authority, and against lawful authority, incur the penalty and risk of perishing by the sword. This meaning seems to be attached to those words by the occasion and circumstances which prompted them. If understood in their unlimited latitude, they would contradict the experience and testimony of all ages, it being manifest that many military men die peaceably in their beds." ³

As Jay noted, Christ's mission precluded the use of force in this particular instance, nonetheless, Jesus taught the legitimacy of using the legal sword to restrain the illegal sword of an aggressor. Peter here however, in his impatience became the aggressor rather than remaining in the posture of self-defense.

The Bible states that the authority and responsibility of using the sword to punish evil or protect the righteous (either from within a nation or from aggression by an outside enemy) resides with the civil government (Rom. 13:1-4). [This does not negate the Scriptural right to use force to protect ourselves and our families from personal harm.] That is why anytime we reach the step where force is necessary in resisting tyranny, we must go through legitimate governing officials. A lower representative must be convinced to ignore a higher decree and declare that a higher ruler is acting in rebellion to God's higher law. This is the theory of **interposition** which is based in Scripture and was affirmed by Manegold in 1080 and again in the Protestant Reformation of Europe. One of the best treatises on it was written by the French Protestants in 1579 entitled *A Defense of Liberty Against Tyrants.*

In the American Christian Revolution, the colonists were not in rebellion (from God's perspective) in their struggle for independence from Britain, but were acting in accordance with the Biblical guidelines for resisting tyranny. They followed the above three steps in order. If we do not follow these steps in order, we will bring undue harm to ourselves, to others, and to God's cause. But those who do follow God's guidelines properly and

87

disobey an ungodly law or ruler must be prepared to pay the price for such an action, recognizing permanent change will come gradually as more people are changed from within. Some may have to suffer while this is taking place.

Thus, we see that Jesus Christ, the focal point of all human history, is also the turning point in the history of liberty. He provided the basis for internal liberty with His sacrificial death for sin. But He also provided an extensive set of teachings on external liberty which was part of what He wanted taught among the nations when He gave His disiples the Great Commission: *"Go therefore and make disciples of all the nations...,teaching them to observe all things that I have commanded you.."* (Mt 28:19,20).

The Essential Foundations & Structures of Christian Nations

The following chapters deal with the essential foundations and structures of Christian nations. The principles examined in Chapter 1 must be infused into the lives of the citizens of a nation desiring to be free, just, and prosperous. It is in the homes, educational institutions, churches, and media outlets that these principles are imparted. If these institutions do not fulfill their God-given purposes and responsibilities, the citizens will lack the necessary character and understanding to support the structures of a Godly nation and the result will be bondage, injustice, and poverty.

The Four Basic Spheres of Responsibility and Jurisdictional Authority

The following chart briefly summarizes the purpose and responsibilities of individuals and the divine institutions which God established. The following chapters will look at some aspects of this chart in more detail. It is not within the scope of this book to examine the role of prayer and personal devotion in building a Christian nation. These are obviously of first importance, but since many good books have been written on these topics and this is usually the emphasis of most church and missionary work, we felt the needed information could be obtained elsewhere. However, as is repeatedly stated in this book, change begins in the heart of man and nations undergo Godly transformation only from the internal to the external.

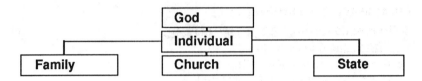

Individual

Purpose and Responsibilities:

1. Worship -- Loving our God (Luke 10:27, Deut. 6:5)

    * Love God with all our heart, soul, mind, and strength

  a. Personal prayer, Bible reading/study/meditation...

  b. Assemble with others

  c. Sabbath observance

2. Charity -- Loving our neighbor (Luke 10:27, Lev. 19:9-18, Mt. 25:35-36)

    * Golden rule: Do unto others as you would have them do unto you

  a. Assist the needy and show mercy

  b. Speak the truth -- evangelism, exhortation, edification

  c. Involvement in society/government [conversion of institutions]

3. Work -- Loving ourself (Gen. 1:26-28, 2:15)

    * Be fruitful and subdue earth; cultural mandate; fulfilling our calling

  a. Provide for self and family -- individuals will start businesses and create wealth

  b. Bless the nations -- occurs as individuals provide needed goods and services

Family

A family is simply a man, woman, children who are related by marriage, blood, or adoption. The ideal marriage has a man and woman who covenant together to fulfill God's desire for them to be fruitful and bless the world. Both parents are to fulfill the purpose and responsibilities. In this context fathers (in general, but not exclusively) lead in society, while mothers raise the next generations. (Gen. 1:18,22-24; 3:16)

Purpose and Responsibilities:

1. Procreation (Gen. 1:28, 1 Tim. 5:10,14)
* Be fruitful and multiply
a. Pro-life -- sanctity of life (Gen. 9:6)
b. Children -- a blessing (Ps. 127:3-5)

2. Education (Dt. 6:6-7)
* "You shall teach your sons"
a. Fit children to fulfill their individual purposes and responsibilities (Pr. 22:6)
b. Build Godly character (Gen. 18:19)
c. Train in a Biblical world-view (Ps. 78:5)
d. Discipline as well as instruction (Eph. 6:4)

3. Health and Welfare
* Practice hospitality, especially for those of your own household.
a. Preventative health care -- proper exercise, nutrition, sanitation
b. Taking care of the sick, elderly, orphan, widow (1 Tim. 5:4,8,10,16; Dt. 15:7,8,11; Dt. 14:28-29)
c. Saving and investing for your retirement and your posterity (2 Cor. 12:14, Pr. 19:14, Dt. 21:17)

Church

* The church prepares people who govern society.

Purpose and Responsibilities:

1. Regular instruction of members in Biblical truth for every sphere of life
a. Via Sunday preaching, regular classes, and other educational means (Mt. 28:18-20, 2 Tim. 3:16-17)
b. Includes starting schools and colleges

2. Administer Sacraments and Church Discipline (1 Cor. 5:8-13; 11:23-25; Mt. 18:15-17)
a. Corporate worship and sacrifice (Gen. 4:3-5,26)
b. Baptism and Lord's Supper (communion)
c. Excommunication

3. Discipling, equipping, and organizing believers (Eph. 4:11-12,16; Titus 3:8,14)

   a. Providing coordination and support for individuals and families to work in voluntary union with others to fulfill their purpose
   b. Pastors are to be role models in their personal conduct and through their involvement in society of what the church teaches.

Civil Government (State)

Purpose and Responsibilities:

1. Protect the righteous, i.e. law-abiding citizens (Rom. 13:3-4, 1 Pet. 2:13-14)

Protection of life, liberty, and property from domestic and foreign lawbreakers. (Governments are to secure God-given inalienable rights.)

a. Life	Liberty	Property
Ex. 20:13 - "You shall not murder"	Ex. 21:6 -- "He who kidnaps a man...shall be put to death."	Ex. 20:15 -- "You shall not steal."
Self-defense	Free worship	Private property
Govt protection	Free speech	Individual enterprise
	Free assembly	Acquire necessities of life
	Free press	
	Free schools	
	Right to petition government	

   b. Government coordinates civilian police for order and army for defense.
   c. Protection of rights from government abuse as well, via:
   Decentralize government
   Separation of powers
   Election of representatives

2. Punish the evil doer, i.e. criminal (Ex. 20:13; 21:12; 22:2)

   a. Set up Constitution with just laws and death penalty
   b. Impartial judges and fair trial to establish justice

Chapter 7

The Principle Approach to Education - Developing Citizens with a Biblical Worldview

The philosophy of education in one generation will be the philosophy of government in the next generation.

As the father of the American Revolution, Samuel Adams knew what it would take to renovate a nation. He said:

"Let divines and philosophers, statesmen and patriots, unite their endeavors to renovate the age, by impressing the minds of men with the importance of educating their little boys and girls, of inculcating in the minds of youth the fear and love of the Deity and universal philanthropy, and, in subordination to these great principles, the love of their country; of instructing them in the art of self-government, without which they never can act a wise part in the government of societies, great or small; in short, of leading them in the study and practice of the exalted virtues of the Christian system ..." [1]

Tyranny is the result of ignorance. Benjamin Franklin said: *"A nation of well informed men who have been taught to know and prize the rights which God has given them cannot be enslaved. It is in the region of ignorance that tyranny begins."*

93

Much of the Western "Christian" world has become secularized in recent generations. One primary reason this has occurred is that Christians have lost a biblical world-view, and hence have acted, or failed to act, accordingly. Their ignorance of the truth has shifted the general direction of Western culture, from the path of liberty, justice, and prosperity (the fruit of the gospel) to tyranny, oppression, and lack (the fruit of humanism and secularism). Many nations are just beginning down this path (the influence of Christianity still has much positive influence) and don't recognize the end result of basing a nation on secular ideas. A great number that have operated on such ideas (for example, many former communist nations) are looking to instill Christianity in the life of their nations.

A biblical world-view and a providential view of history (at least to some degree) predominated in the thinking of the church and the western world from just after the Reformation until the 20th Century. The degree to which various nations adhered to biblical truth varied, but they were at least on the right path. Those who founded the United States of America had a biblical world-view, including the non-Christians (such as Franklin and Jefferson), while today a secular or humanistic world-view predominates, even among many Christians.

Education has played a key role in this secularization. One of the seven principles of liberty is the principle of Christian education. This is how biblical truth is passed on to our children and others.

A Christian Philosophy, Methodology, and Curriculum

"Christian" means "that which pertains to Christ." As all aspects of education must pertain to Christ for education to be Christian, the following must pertain to Christ in Christian education:

1) Philosophy - why (also who, when, where),
2) Methodology - how,
3) Curriculum - what.

Many "Christian" schools and churches have humanistic philosophy, methodology, and/or curriculum.

What is Education?

Colossians 2:8 tells us that a worldly philosophy brings captivity:

"See to it that no one takes you captive through philosophy and empty deception, according to the tradition of men, according to the elementary principles of the world, rather than according to Christ."

A wordly, humanistic philosophy in the present educational system of many nations has produced bondage within individuals' lives.

While a worldly philosophy brings captivity, the Bible tells us that a Christian philosophy brings liberty. In order to liberate a nation, individuals must be liberated first. True education is the primary means of imparting a Christian philosophy of life, and hence in bringing liberty to our nation.

In order to properly educate ourselves, we must first understand what true education is. If we were to define education from our experience in public schools, we would probably agree with most modern dictionary definitions of the word, which define it as teaching that primarily is concerned with imparting information. Education does involve imparting information, but according to the Bible this is of secondary concern.

Noah Webster, in his original *American Dictionary of the English Language* (1828), reveals to us four minimal goals of education. He writes: *"Education comprehends all that series of instruction and discipline which is intended to:*

[1.] enlighten the understanding,

[2.] correct the temper,

[3.] form the manners and habits of youth, and

[4.] fit them for usefulness in their future stations."[2]

We can see from his definition that education deals primarily with the inward man - with forming character. The formation of character is inevitable. Bad character, not good, is the result of the failure of public schools to discipline and provide moral education.

Not only is the forming of good character neglected, but schools (including colleges) fail in the majority of areas of study to fit students for usefulness in their future stations. Upon completing school, most individuals lack creativity and entrepreneurship, for most of their educational experience was as a consumer of knowledge. True education must build producers - those who are able to take the knowledge they have and apply it to many new areas without someone always telling them step by step what to do.

The root of the word "education" has a dual meaning of "to pour in" and "to draw out." Both teaching (pouring in) and learning (drawing out) are involved in true education. Not only should we pour information and knowledge into a child, but we must make sure that we understand and know how to practically apply that which is taught. Education has not occurred until the students start producing.

There are a number of reasons why we should educate our children - it builds character, it enables progress to occur, and it keeps us from destroying ourselves (Hos. 4:6). In addition, God commands us to educate our children (see Chapter 8), and He commands the Church to educate the nations (Mt. 28:18-20). Education is a vital part of the gospel.

Discovering a Biblical Method of Education

Having seen what biblical education is and agreeing that it is important, we must now ask: "How should we educate? Is there a Christian method of education?"

To answer that question, we must first understand that methods are not neutral. Paul instructed the church at Corinth to be careful how they built upon the foundation he laid for the church (1 Cor. 3:10), for he understood that how you build something is just as important as what you build.

We would readily agree that the content of the material taught in public schools is thoroughly humanistic and quite destructive of the godly character and thought in our youth (which in turn is destructive of our religious and political freedom and happiness). Not only is the content humanistic (and thus, destructive), but the method employed to teach these ideas is also humanistic and probably just as destructive as the content, if not more so. For example, television is used as a method of communicating information to our youth (and to ourselves). It takes little discernment to recognize that the content of most television programs is ungodly. Violence, immorality, anti-traditional values, and blatant and subtle humanistic ideas dominate the airwaves. As bad as the content is, the method is probably worse. What does a child do as he sits for hours everyday in front of the television? The answer is nothing! His imagination, creativity and faculties of reasoning are not developed. Study after study has revealed that the more television a child watches, the poorer he does academically.

Using a biblical method to teach our children is essential if we desire to achieve our intended results. David and Israel of old learned the hard way that how you do something is just as important as what you desire to do.

During David's reign as king, he had a good idea: "Let us bring back the ark of our God to us, for we did not seek it in the days of Saul" (1 Chron.13:3).

Twenty years earlier, the Philistines had captured the ark of God during a battle with Israel. Now David desired to bring the ark into the holy city of Jerusalem. This was an excellent idea, but how he went about it proved of the utmost importance. Uzza would definitely testify to that truth, if we could talk to him today.

As the ark was being transported from Abinadab's house on a cart, it was almost upset. Yet Uzza came to the rescue and reached out his hand to steady the ark. But this was the last thing Uzza did, for God struck him down and he died.

David sought out the truth from God's word and discovered that using a cart to transport the ark was not God's way to move it, but the Philistine's way (1 Chron.15). He learned that **there is a danger in trying to do what is right in the wrong way.**

In educating our children, we must seek to not only build what God wants, but to do it in the way he wants.

Being a Christian does not necessarily make one a Christian teacher. Not only must the reasons and motives for teaching (the philosophy) and the content of what is taught (the curriculum) be of Christ, but the method of teaching must be Christian as well in order for a truly Christian education to be provided. Taking humanistic methods or curricula and throwing in a few scriptures and a prayer does not make for instruction Christian. A candy-coated gospel method is not sufficient to build men and women of Christian character and thought.

The Principle Approach to Education

If methods are not neutral and there is a Christian method of education, then what is that method? It is what has been called the Principle Approach. Briefly stated, the Principle Approach to education inculcates in individuals the ability to reason from the Bible to every aspect of life. As Christians, we know we are supposed to do this, but do we? Do we really know how to reason from the Bible to geography, astronomy, mathematics, or history, not to mention national defense, foreign policy, or civil government?

The Principle Approach restores the art of biblical reasoning. Many Christians of recent generations have read Romans 12:2 as follows: "Do not be conformed to this world, but be transformed by the *removal* of your mind..." We know that we are transformed by the *renewing* of our mind and not by its *removal*, yet many Christians over-responded to the decay of the

97

institutionalized church in past generations into a mental religion only by rejecting the use of our minds in following God, desiring only to be "led by the Spirit".

We must again realize that as Christians we have the potential to be the greatest thinkers in all the world. Historically, Christians have been the leaders in almost every area of life (e.g. Johann S. Bach in music, Isaac Newton in science, Rembrandt in art, Adam Smith in economics, John Locke in civil government). To bring freedom, justice, advancement, and prosperity to nations today will require men who know how to reason biblically to all areas of life.

Most of the activities that are sweeping many nations today teach people not to think. Billions of dollars are spent on video games each year, with billions more spent on movies, sports, and other games. Amusement, which is derived from "a" and "muse", meaning "not thinking", is an apt description of these activities.

We are in great need today of restoring the art of biblical reasoning to our educational system. We may have more facts taught in our schools today (even though in many fields, major facts are conspicuously missing), but we must teach more than just facts. We must teach how to arrive at those facts as well.

To more fully understand the Principle Approach, let's look at each of the words separately. A "principle", according to Webster's 1828 dictionary, is: "1) The cause, source, or origin of anything; that from which a thing proceeds; 2) Element; constituent part."

A principle is like an element in chemistry. An element is the lowest form in which matter can exist naturally - it can be broken down no further. A principle is an absolute truth (and hence, biblical) that is reduced to its most basic form. While the Bible contains thousands of truths, these can be broken down into a small number of principles from which the truths spring forth. If these principles are known, this provides complete parameters through which to view life, assuring that one truth is not forgotten while embracing a new one.

A "principle" and a "seed" are very similar in their meanings. A seed, being a plant in embryo, contains the entire plant - the whole thing is there, albeit in a condensed form. After a seed is planted, given some time, water, sunlight, and care, a huge tree can be produced. Likewise, principles are first given in seed form to children, yet these principles contain the potential of giant trees of truth and application. God starts with a seed and produces a plant. Today, most classes try to shove plants down children's throats.

The Principle Approach teaches seed principles over and over again in each subject and grade level with different illustrations, examples, assignments, educational methods, etc. This ensures that a child not only knows biblical principles, but that he lives them - that they are a part of his life.

"Approach" simply means "to come or go near, in place; to draw near." Therefore, the principle approach involves getting the principles so near someone that they become a part of their life.

The principle approach involves reasoning from the root or seed or principle to the facts or issues. Education should not involve only memorizing all the facts. This is just as true for the church in her addressing issues of the day as it is for children studying in school.

This explains why on some issues many Christians have completely opposite viewpoints (e.g. the church's involvement in civil government), yet God has only one view of these situations, which we must understand if we desire to provide solutions for these difficult problems. Christians on both sides of the issues claim to have the Bible as their base of belief, so why do they have opposite views? It is because they are not reasoning from the same biblical principles.

Taking a few scriptures and forming an opinion on a subject is not sufficient. We must reason from the totality of the Bible, not violating any principle while seemingly adhering to the truth based on a few scriptures. If our conclusion on any issue violates any principle, then we can know it is wrong. Yet conversely, if our conclusion agrees with the foundational principles, this does not assure us that it is correct owing to our limited knowledge of the extent of these foundational principles. The more understanding we have of these principles, the more likely it will be that our view is correct.

A Wholistic Method

The Principle Approach is also a wholistic method of education, that is, it is instruction from the whole to the part. We will use history as an example. Instead of teaching fragments of history throughout the various grade levels with seemingly no unifying factor among the different classes, a biblical approach would look at the whole of history first and then look at the parts in more detail, and those always in relation to the whole.

The whole of history can be looked at from a biblical philosophy because there is an overall purpose in history which unifies all the specific events of history. From a humanistic viewpoint, there is no purpose in history, and hence, no unifying theme which ties events of history together.

This overall view and purpose of history is taught to a child from the very beginning of his schooling. He is given the overall picture to begin with, and then as he advances, the parts can be looked at in more detail. He will have an overall framework in which to put all the information he learns.

Not only are the events of history centered around God and His Son Jesus, but the origin, development, and purpose of all fields of knowledge are directly related to God's plan in the earth.

As this is understood, there will be a reference in which all information logically fits; hence, learning will not just involve memorizing a number of facts.

A truly biblical approach to education involves much more than just taking various academic subjects and trying to squeeze the Bible into them. A biblical principled approach to education will reveal that the source, origin, and purpose of all knowledge revolves around God and His plan for man.

How Do We Implant Principles?

If we desire to have a Principle Approach education, we must restore the 4 R's to teaching and learning:

1) First R - RESEARCH: We must research the subjects and topics of interest from the Bible and other resources to identify basic principles.

2) Second R - REASON: As we are researching a subject, we must continually ask ourselves what is God's perspective and purpose for the subject and what does this information reveal to me of God and His purpose.

3) Third R - RELATE: As we are researching and reasoning, we must also relate the truths uncovered to our own lives or to the situation at hand.

4) Fourth R - RECORD: The principles and truths uncovered and related must be recorded or written down to accurately and permanently preserve them. [3]

This process of researching, reasoning, relating, and recording ("4-Ring") is the best way to implant truth within our hearts - the best method by which to learn and be educated.

In most schools (and certainly most churches) today, students are seldom required to research, reason, relate or record in their pursuit of being educated. This is true in the everyday study of subjects as well as the tests on the subjects. Most tests are fill-in-the-blank, matching, or True-False. Students can take and pass these test for years and years without truly learning how to reason and think and be prepared for life after completion of school. Consequently, far too many people today do not know how to reason and think.

Practical Ways to Implement the 4 R's in our Educational Process

1) Essays

Writing essays is an excellent way to implant within the student the ability to research, reason, relate, and record. Writing essays enables students to truly express themselves - to communicate what they really know and believe. As one writes his ideas in complete sentences, he is forced to reason and think for himself. This personal expression brings liberty to the individual. He will not be dependent upon the media, teachers, or anyone else for his ideas, for he will have learned how to search out the truth for himself.

2) Notebooks

The compilation of notebooks by students on various subjects and topics is an excellent means of inculcating truth within them. Instead of being handed a textbook at the beginning of the year and memorizing pages of facts and information, in order to receive good grades, the student develops his own textbook by taking notes from the teacher and doing his own research and writing from various resources (which can include a textbook).

The notebook method not only assures that the student acquires knowledge, but it also builds character within the individual (which is the primary purpose of education). Self-government, industry, orderliness, discipline, and the ability to communicate and reason are only a few of the character qualities produced by the notebook method of education.

America's founding fathers were educated by the notebook method. Many of George Washington's early notebooks are still preserved in the Library of Congress. His life-time habits of orderliness, neatness, and consistency are readily seen within the pages of his manuscripts. His father required this of him from his first years of being educated.

In a letter to his father on June 2, 1777, at age 10, John Quincy Adams wrote:

> *"P.S. -Sir, If you will be so good as to favor me with a blank-book I will transcribe the most remarkable occurrences I meet with in my reading, which will serve to fix them upon my mind."*[A]

This is quite an amazing statement for a ten-year old, not only in that his literary level is beyond most college graduates today, but also in his educational insight. America's future sixth president was revealing the importance of a notebook approach to education.

There are many other practical educational methods that can be used to restore the 4-R's. Some include:

1) Verbal reports and tests
2) Complete sentences answers to classroom and test questions
3) Practical outlets for expression of all that is learned
4) Apprenticeship programs
5) Doing useful projects within the various classes

You can begin to see that a principle approach to education requires much work. While true education will be exciting and challenging, and not boring (one reason for the many discipline problems in schools today is that students are extremely bored), it will also require severe effort.

If you have not exercised in many years and then participate in strenuous activity, your body will hurt. Likewise, if you haven't exercised your mind for years and begin to use it strenuously, it will also hurt. But the more you use your mind, the better in shape you will be to think.

Your mind is more than just a computer - garbage in, garbage out. It is like a womb, for you can get more out of your mind than you put in it. This is part of true reasoning.

Three Essentials for Christian Education

To sum up what has been stated previously, these three elements are essential for an education to be truly Christian:

1) Teacher - A teacher who is a living witness or textbook (2 Cor. 3:3) is the most important aspect of education. When you teach, you impart more of who you are than what you know. Students will read you. Therefore, to be most effective as a teacher (we are all teachers, for we instruct all with whom we come in contact), you must master what you teach so that it is a living part of you.

2) Content - In the material we teach, the Bible must be our central text (as we have discussed, not in a superficial way). While the Bible doesn't contain all the facts on all the subjects, it does contain all the principles and reveals God's purpose for each subject.

3) Method - In addition to a godly teacher and content, the educational method must also be Christian. This method should build godly character, impart a love of learning, and prepare individuals to take dominion over the earth.

In light of what we have discussed in this chapter, as we look at public education in the past few generations in many nations and see the humanistic philosophy which permeates those systems, it is no wonder that the laws are becoming more and more ungodly. Today, humanists, marxists and others are using public school rooms as their pulpits to propagate their religion.

This is especially true in America, who had biblical law as its base, but is now shifting to man-centered evolving law. America's founding fathers recognized that the godly ideals and character which gave birth to that nation must be perpetuated in the homes and in the educational institutions if America was to prosper and remain free. They saw that Christianity must be the foundation for all education.

As Rosalie Slater writes:

"American Christian education was the foundation of our nation's great growth, progress and success. The rise of the individual in our country and his freedom to conduct his affairs in the matter of his own choosing was the direct outcome of expression in American life of 'the Christian idea of man.'

"The colonists brought with them a tradition of Biblical scholarship and the fruition of the Reformation - the Scriptures in English. And with their Bibles they brought a determination to continue the individual study and practice of the Christian verities contained therein. Because of their sincere desire to teach their children to read the Scriptures they established schools. Their colleges were the culmination of the need for an enlightened ministry.

"Historically American education had its basis for both a sound Christian foundation and a curriculum which had both academic and literary excellence." [5]

Biblical Scholarship

What was this "Biblical Scholarship" that formed the basis for all education in America for well over half centuries? Simply stated, Biblical Scholarship is the ability to reason from Biblical principles and relate it to all of life. Not only did early American Christians reason from the Bible, but even non-Christians were trained in this manner and held to a Biblical worldview. This is quite the opposite of today for both non-Christians and even many Christians view life from a man-centered, humanistic worldview. Decades of humanistic teaching in schools and by the media have attempted to engrain this philosophy in all Americans.

What is a World View?

Gary Demar writes that *"a world view is simply the way you look at yourself and the world around you. It includes your beliefs about God, yourself, your neighbors, your family, civil government, art, music, history, morality, education, business, economics and all other areas of life."*

Ron Jenson says: *"Your world view, of course, is how you view the world. It is the set of presuppositions - that which is believed beforehand - which underlies all of our decisions and actions. These presuppositions (our world view) determine our thinking patterns, which in turn influence our actions . . . Our world view may be conscious or unconscious, but it determines our destiny and the destiny of the society we live in."*

It was the biblical world-view and scholarship of Colonial Americans that provided the basis of a free and prosperous America. How could the Pilgrims, a mere group of farmers and common laborers, write the historically significant Mayflower Compact, draw up a peace treaty with the Indians that lasted decades, and institute individual enterprise among them? They could because they knew how to apply the truth of the Bible, not only to "divine things", but also to civil affairs.

Families, Churches, and Schools all passed on this ability to reason from the Bible and apply it to all of life. This accounts for the excellent quality of education in early America. One only needs to read an excerpt from a sermon or newspaper to realize their level of literacy was much higher than even college graduates receive today. Not only was the level of literacy higher, but the percentage of the population who were literate was also higher.

The Need for Christianity in Our Schools

A godly nation must rest upon a Christian philosophy of education. American historian B.F. Morris says in his history:

> *"Education, next to the Christian religion, is an indispensable element of republican institutions, the basis upon which all free governments must rest. The state must rest upon the basis of religion, and it must preserve this basis, or itself must fall. But the support which religion gives to the state will obviously cease the moment religion loses its hold upon the popular mind. The very fact that state must have religion as a support for its own authority demands that some means for teaching religion be employed. Better for it to give up all other instruction than that religion should be disregarded in its schools."[6]*

In America the foundational religion was Christianity. Her liberty, growth, and prosperity was the result of a biblical philosophy of life. Her continued freedom and success is dependent upon Americans educating their youth in the principles of the Christian religion. This applies to all nations that desire liberty.

Noah Webster understood this as he wrote:

> *"The foundation of all free government and of all social order must be laid in families and in the discipline of youth. . . The Education of youth, an employment of more consequence than making laws and preaching the gospel because it lays the foundation on which both law and gospel rest for success..."[7]*

How we educate our youth has immeasurable consequences for the future of our nation.

Chapter 8

The Home and the School

The Foundation of a Free State Rests in the Home

The family is the basic building block of society. As is the family in a nation, so is the church, state, education, business, arts, and life of that nation. The home is the first sphere of society and not only determines the foundation of these components of society, but also determines the extent to which they prosper.

The moral problems which plague the nations today may be attributed to neglect of the young by parents. It is in the home where people are instilled with godly character and a biblical world-view, both of which are necessary to support free, just, and prosperous nations. The goal of the Christian home in a republic is to love and nurture the young, build individual character, and train future generations to govern the earth.

The foundational principles examined in Chapter 1 are most effectively imparted to the citizens of a nation in the homes. It is here that individuals first learn the outworking of their faith and put into practice the biblical principles that support free nations.

What Rosalie Slater writes about America applies to any nation:

"There are few statements today about the opportunity and the obligation of a Christian home in a republic. Yet there is no single element in America which contributes more significantly to the success of Christian Constitutional government. It is in the home where the foundations of Christian character are laid. It is in the home where Christian self-government is learned and practiced. Yet, the Christian American who is aware of the particular

challenges to America's Christian character and to the Constitutional form of government still inclines to political education outside the home. Thus, while parents are active politically, educationally, religiously, it becomes necessary for other agencies--the school, the church, the community--to pick up the responsibility for making home the first sphere of government in the republic. Needless to say they cannot substitute what only the home can provide." [1]

As Christians seek to reform the nations, they must never underestimate the importance of the family in the life of the nations. In no area should greater attention be paid than to the nature, responsibilities, duties, and influences of the home. The beginning of preparing the way for Christ to gain preeminence in a nation includes turning "the hearts of the fathers back to their children, and the hearts of the children to their fathers" (Malachi 4:6, Luke 1:17), the lack of which brings a curse upon the land.

What is the Home or Family?

The true idea of home is realized only in context of Christianity. The family is a divine institution of God and will only succeed as family members seek to apply His principles in the home. Some of the biblical principles which will cause homes to flourish include:

1. The marriage union is sacred. Once entered into, there will be no thought of divorce or adultery, nor desire to act in any way that would destroy that union.

2. Women are raised to their proper role. Historically, it has been the influence of Christianity that has elevated women above the role of servants or second class citizens. In Christian homes, husbands will treat wives as Christ treats the church (Ephesians 5:25).

3. The true family is united by the bond of Christ. The love within such a family is self-denying. Members of the home will have a greater concern for others than for themselves and will possess a love that is stronger than death (Philippians 2:3-11). Such homes will not be destroyed. Without the bond of Christ to unite the family, only natural affection holds it together, which is not enough, as evidenced by the growth of divorce in many nations today.

4. Christian parents see children as a gift of the Lord (Psalms 127:3), and themselves as stewards. They are to prepare their children to love and obey God, to seek to live as He commands, and to fulfill His will for their lives. In the home is the first church, the first school, the first business, and the first government. Here people develop character and knowledge, have ministry, learn of work, and learn how to govern their lives and lead others.

God must be the center of the home, and His principles must be the basis for the family if it is to fulfill its central role in the life of a nation. Parents cannot just think of the home as a refuge from the world or as a place to escape and relax. God has divinely established the family and gives children to parents as part of His plan for them and the nations.

A monument in Plymouth, Massachusetts known as The Pilgrim Mother contains this inscription:

"They brought up their families in sturdy virtue and a living faith in God without which nations perish."

Without the home fulfilling this role, no nation can long endure.

The Mission of the Christian Home

As the God-ordained basic building block of society, homes have been given by God the general mission to provide the "temporal and eternal well-being of its members". In early life, children are completely dependent upon their parents for all their needs. God expects parents to provide the physical, mental, moral, and spiritual needs of their children. Those parents who do not are "worse than an infidel" (1 Timothy 5:8). Our natural affections will prompt us to do this, but we have need of God's word to understand how to do this properly and completely.

Parents should meet the needs of their children (physical, mental, moral, emotional, and spiritual) until they have trained their children to provide for themselves. Neglect of any of their needs, or failure to train them to provide their own needs and the needs of their future families, is wrong and will result in problems, not only for the child in later life, but also for the society in which they live.

As an example: Up until 1959, only 2% of children of black families in the United States were raised by single parents. Today over 50% of black children are raised by single parents. What is the result of this? (The cause of this is another question.) One must merely look at the inner cities and see the exponential increase of crime, drugs, murder, etc. to see the fruit of broken homes.

109

Concerning the care of their children, parents are to be faithful stewards to God, to Whom we all belong. God says to such parents: *"Go nurse them for the King of Heaven, and He will pay thee hire."*[2]

Parents must realize that they are equipping their children for temporal life on earth **and** for life eternal. Lack of proper training will cause those in later life to look back at their youthful home with sorrow.

The primary duties of a Christian home are to teach the Bible, seek God in prayer and worship, maintain discipline, build Christian character, and impart a biblical view of life, for if we train our children rightly, they will not depart from it (Proverbs 22:6). We can expect non-Christians to be worldly, but if Christian families are as well, then the nation they represent is doomed to perish.

If parents see children as playthings or burdens and relegate their up-bringing to others, then parental duty cannot be fulfilled. There is no substitute for the parents - no day-care, school, person, or institution can take the place of Mom or Dad.

It is important to have a regular Sabbath Day for not only attending church but also to have a time at home for "remembering" God's hand in the history of your family, church and nation (Deut 5:15). In addition to this, there should be a regular Bible devotional time and reading aloud from classic Christian literature.

Influence of the Home

The influence of the home can be summarized in two points:

1. The home molds the character and shapes the destiny of men.

Men of great character and influence, from Timothy (2 Timothy 1:5), Augustine, and John Wesley to George Washington and Abraham Lincoln, have repeatedly acknowledged the home as the source of who they were and what they accomplished.

2. The home determines the course of a nation.

That which shapes men, shapes the nation. The influence of the character and ideas instilled in men through the home is evidenced in the governments, schools, churches, media, and businesses of the nations. We will have good citizens when we have good parents. Napoleon understood this when he said, *"What France wants is good mothers, and you may be sure then that France*

110

will have good sons." [3] The Christian home produced the founders of the United States of America, who established the first Christian republic, with all its attendant blessings and liberty, which in turn has influenced liberty in all the world.

The Home Is the Primary Place of Education

The Bible teaches that the home is the primary institution for training the future generations. The father, mother and grandparents are all to take part in the education of the youth.

Ephesians 6:1-4 tells us that the **father** is especially important in the education of children. Verse 4 says: *"Fathers, provoke not your children to wrath: but bring them up in the nurture and admonition of the Lord."* The word nurture means "to train, to educate, to tutor; to personally have input in a child." Fathers must take time to personally train and educate their children.

The Bible also commands parents to diligently teach the truth to their children (Deuteronomy 6:4-6). God chose Abraham to be a father of nations because he knew he would be faithful to train his children (Genesis 18:19). Solomon, through the book of Proverbs, not only instructed his children but has also been able to instruct multitudes of youth over the centuries. It was his father's instruction that enabled him to do this.

A primary role of **mothers** is to teach (Proverbs 1:8; Titus 2:3). The chapter in Proverbs that has taught multitudes the characteristics of a virtuous woman was written by a man, King Lemuel. He learned this from his mother (Proverbs 31).

American statesman Daniel Webster said:

"The domestic hearth is the first of schools and the best of lecture-rooms; for there the heart will co-operate with the mind, the affections with the reasoning powers, And this is the scene for the almost exclusive sway of woman. Yet, great as their influence thus exercised undoubtedly is, it escapes observation in such a manner that history rarely takes much account of it. . . . The mothers of a civilized nation. . . work, not on frail and perishable materials, but on the immortal mind, molding and fashioning beings who are to exist forever. They work, not upon the canvas that shall perish, or the marble that shall crumble into dust, but upon mind, upon spirit, which is to last forever, and which is to bear, for good or evil, throughout its duration,

111

the impress of a mother's. . . hand. . . that in a free republic woman performs her sacred duty and fulfills her destiny.''[A]

Mrs. Lydia Sigourney, a pioneer in education for women, said:

"The natural vocation of females is to teach. . . . It is in the domestic sphere, in her own native province, that woman is inevitably a teacher. . . . This influence is most visible and operative in a republic. . . . Teachers under such a form of government should be held in the highest honor. They are the allies of legislators. They have agency in the prevention of crime. They aid in regulating the atmosphere, whose incessant action and pressure causes the life blood to circulate, and return pure healthful to the heart of the nation. . . . Demand of her as a debt the highest excellence of which she is capable of attaining. Summon her to abandon selfish motives and inglorious ease. Incite her to those virtues which promote the permanence and health of nations. Make her accountable for the character of the next generation. Give her solemn charge in the presence of men and of angels. Gird her with the whole armor of education and piety, and see if she be not faithful to her children, to her country, and to her God. . . for the strength of a nation, especially of a republican nation, is in the intelligent and well-ordered homes of the people."[5]

Grandparents should also take part in the education of the youth (Deuteronomy 4:9). Timothy attributes his Christian education to his mother and grandmother (2 Tim. 1:5; 3:14-17) since his father was a pagan (Acts 16:3). Teaching by grandparents not only benefits their grandchildren but it also is a help to them. Over the years they have acquired much wisdom and knowledge that the youth need. In addition, it gives them a sense of usefulness.

Parents must assume their responsibility to educate their children. If aspects of the child's education are delegated to others, it is still the responsibility of the parents to seek out good tutors or schools that will do the job in the same manner they would.

The **Church also has a role in education** as an extension of the family's responsibility. As the Church goes into all the world to disciple the nations, an integral part of this will involve education (Mt. 28:18-20). We have already seen that education of the common man has accompanied the spread of the gospel in history.

The State Is Not Responsible for Training and Educating the Youth.
The only mention of state education in the Bible is in Daniel, where Babylon is indoctrinating the Hebrew youth in its statist ideas. God condemns this education (see Dan. 1:3-6). The more the state assumes this responsibility (which is usually as parents give it up), the more they attempt to act as the home, and hence, destroy the base of happiness in a society. As we have said, the state never makes a good mom and dad. Biblically, the state is given the responsibility to protect and defend its citizens. Education in relation to this activity is needed and welcomed.

The Role of the School

The role of the school in a nation should simply be an extension of the educational role of the home. Where there are Christian homes, there will be Christian schools, assuming there is freedom to establish schools. If there is no freedom, the rise in Christian homes will produce men of character and wisdom, who will work to change the government and laws which will allow freedom to educate in the home and school.

Educational Examples from History

Israel vs. Pagan nations
Jewish children were taught in the home until age eight. Then some of them, as a supplement to home training, were tutored by the Levites and priests until approximately 13 years old (Gal. 4; 2 Chron 17:7-9). They were taught to read at age five. Pagan children received education only if they were children of royalty or elite classes, and it usually occurred outside of the home by the state.

Christianity reforms pagan educational methods.
In the first centuries of the Christian era, the Christian homes adopted the Jewish model of education. As the Church backslid, they adopted the pagan philosophy of education - that education is only for a select few, the clergy. This is one cause of bondage and ignorance of the people during the Middle Ages.

John Wycliffe of England translated the Scriptures in common English in 1382, and his itinerant preachers known as Lollards distributed them. They then began to teach the people how to read so they could learn the Scriptures. Prior to this, only priests and noblemen could read the Bible.

Education Spread During the Reformation

Education in most of Europe was corrupt when the Protestant Reformation began. Consequently, Calvin and Luther established new schools in their respective cities. Educational reform was one of the main reasons why the Puritans came to the New World and developed American educational institutions. Cotton Mather wrote:

> *"The schools of learning and religion (in the Old World) are so corrupted as most of the fairest hopes, are perverted, corrupted, and utterly overthrown by the multitude of evil examples and licentious behavior in these seminaries."*[6]

Education of the Common Man

Colonial America was unique in many ways. Each colony desired that every person be educated, not just the rich or a select few as was the case in Europe and the rest of the world. This idea of education for the common man was of Christian origin. Deuteronomy 6 reveals that it is the family's responsibility to educate their children. God wanted ancient Israel to educate every child because the success of their nation depended upon each person knowing and living the truth of God's Word. If the common man lost this truth, the nation lost its freedom and prosperity.

Home Education

Schools were established in early America mainly because the colonists wanted their children to be able to read the Scriptures. These parents saw that it was not the government's but their responsibility to provide Christian education.

For the first 150-200 years of America's history, education was primarily centered in the home. Home education was sometimes supplemented by tutors or schools, but even here the responsibility and bulk of a child's education rested in the home.

The model of education in Colonial America was very similar to the model used by ancient Israel. With both, education was centered in the home. This was solely the case until around the age of eight or nine. At this age, some children had tutors to further instruct them, or an even smaller number attended a school. With the Israelites, the Levites and the Priests were the tutors; with colonial Americans, the ministers were generally the tutors. If there were too many children in the minister's community for him to go into each home to tutor, he would receive a group of children into his home. These were the first "grammar schools" and began in the late 1600's. This would comprise a child's education until around age thirteen when they would enter an apprenticeship program or possibly enroll in a college.

First Free Public Schools

One of the first schools in America outside the home was started in 1636 in Boston, mainly due to Rev. John Cotton's efforts who willed half his property to the school. It was started to provide education for disadvantaged children or those with no parents.

The Christians of Colonial America also saw it as their responsibility to educate the general public. The Great Commission of Matthew 28:19-20, to "disciple the nations" was to be accomplished by "teaching them to observe all that I commanded you." The Chain of Liberty shows that education always accompanies the spread of the gospel. The Lollards are an excellent example. They educated the common people in order that they could read the Scriptures for themselves. Education of the common man also followed the preaching of Luther, Tyndale, Calvin, and other Reformation preachers. The desire to educate every individual accompanied the Pilgrims, Puritans, Quakers, and most other settlers who came to America.

The "Old Deluder Law" of 1647 established the first free public or common schools in America. Historian John Fiske writes:

> *"In 1647 the legislature of Massachusetts enacted a law with the following preamble: 'It being one chief purpose of that old deluder, Satan, to keep men from the knowledge of the Scriptures,' it was therefore ordered that every township containing fifty families or householders should set up a school in which children might be taught to read and write, and that every township containing one hundred families or householders should set up a school in which boys might be fitted for entering Harvard College."*[7]

Wages for the teachers were paid by the parents or the general inhabitants. These public schools were not under the control of a state government board, such as Horace Mann set up in Massachusetts 200 years later. The teacher's curriculum, methodology, and administration were completely under local control.

Free public schools were also established in other towns and cities of New England over the next number of decades, but these always involved a small percentage of those being educated. The private sector, the home, and the church educated the vast majority of pupils. Samuel Blumenfeld writes that *"by 1720 Boston had far more private schools than public ones, and by the close of the American Revolution many towns had no common schools at all."*[8] Pennsylvania and New York had public schools early, like New England, but only in the cities, not in rural areas. There were no public schools in the Southern colonies until 1730, and only five by 1776.

Although public and private schools were established, the home was still where the majority of Colonial Americans were educated even up through the Revolution. Some of America's greatest leaders and thinkers (not just of that era but including recent years) were primarily educated at home. These include such men as George Washington, Thomas Jefferson, James Madison, Benjamin Franklin, Noah Webster, Abraham Lincoln, Thomas Edison, Alexander G. Bell, and many more.

Samuel L. Blumenfeld says:

"Of the 117 men who signed the Declaration of Independence, the Articles of Confederation and the Constitution, one out of three had had only a few months of formal schooling, and only one in four had gone to college. They were educated by parents, church schools, tutors, academies, apprenticeship, and by themselves."[9]

It is this model that must be reclaimed in America and adopted in every other country that wishes to be free.

Chapter 9

The Church

The People make the laws, and the churches make the people.

This statement expresses well the role of the church in a Christian nation. The influence of the church on government should not be that of directly holding power and making civil law as an ecclesiastical body. It should be an influential power, not a positional power.

A French political philosopher, **Alexis de Tocqueville,** came to the United States of America in the 1830's in search of her greatness. After a thorough examination he concluded:

"On my arrival in the United States the religious aspect of the country was the first thing that struck my attention; and the longer I stayed there, the more I perceived the great political consequences resulting from this new state of things.

"Religion in America takes no direct part in the government of society, but it must be regarded as the first of their political institutions; . . . I do not know whether all Americans have a sincere faith in their religion--for who can search the human heart?--but I am certain that they hold it to be indispensable to the maintenance of republican institutions. This opinion is not peculiar to a class of citizens or to a party, but it belongs to the whole nation and to every rank of society.

"The Americans combine the notions of Christianity and of liberty so intimately in their minds that it is impossible to make them conceive the one without the other. . .[1]

"I sought for the greatness and genius of America in her commodious harbors and her ample rivers, and it was not there; in her fertile fields and boundless prairies, and it was not there; in her rich mines and her vast world commerce, and it was not there. Not until I went to the churches of America and heard her pulpits aflame with righteousness did I understand the secret of her genius and power. America is great because she is good and if America ever ceases to be good, America will cease to be great."[2]

In other words, De Tocqueville said that a Christian civil government will not work without the people being virtuous, which is a product of the religious influence of the church.

How the Clergy Should Disciple the Nation in Principles of Liberty

The church and clergy should not only train the people concerning their spiritual duties, but also train them to apply biblical truth to all areas of life -- including civil government, education, economics, and law.

In the Hebrew Republic, in the early church era, and in European history, the clergy have done this and changed nations dramatically. Some of the best historical examples are:

1. The Levites
2. Jesus and Paul the Apostle
3. Patrick in Ireland (and his disciples in Scotland and England)
4. Asser with Alfred the Great in England
5. Alcuin with Charlemagne in France
6. The Christian Universities
7. Wycliffe and the Lollards in England
8. Hus and his followers in Czechoslovakia
9. Calvin and the Geneva Academy in Switzerland
10. Most of the Protestant Reformers

In Colonial America, the pulpits were aflame with a biblical worldview. Pastors used every opportunity possible to educate the people in the prin-

118

ciples of liberty. One important means of accomplishing this was the election sermon, which was begun in 1633 and occurred regularly for 250 years.

John Wingate Thornton writes of the Election Sermons and the clergy's influence in early America:

"The clergy were generally consulted by the civil authorities; and not infrequently the suggestions from the pulpit, on election days and other special occasions, were enacted into laws. The statutebook, the reflex of the age, shows this influence. The State was developed out of the Church.

"The annual 'Election Sermon'--a perpetual memorial, continued down through the generations from century to century--still bears witness that our fathers ever began their civil year and its responsibilities with an appeal to Heaven, and recognized Christian morality as the only basis of good laws. . . . The sermon is styled the Election Sermon, and is printed. Every representative has a copy for himself, and generally one or more for the minister or ministers of his town. As the patriots have prevailed, the preachers of each sermon have been the zealous friends of liberty; and the passages most adapted to promote the spread and love of it have been selected and circulated far and wide by means of newspapers, and read with avidity and a degree of veneration on account of the preacher and his election to the service of the day. . . .

"The ministers were now to instruct the people, to reason before them and with them, to appeal to them; and so, by their very position and relation, the people were constituted the judges. They were called upon to decide; they also reasoned; and in this way--as the conflicts in the church respected polity rather than doctrine--the Puritans, and especially the New Englanders, had, from the very beginning, been educated in the consideration of its elementary principles."[3]

Rev. John Witherspoon was a great example of an American minister who directly and indirectly shaped public affairs. He typified the colonial clergy who literally discipled the nation. Witherspoon served as a minister, as President of Princeton College, as a signer of the Declaration of Independence, and on over 100 committees in Congress during our struggle for independence. But his indirect influence through his educational efforts were also awesome. While President of Princeton, he trained not only ministers but leaders in all areas of life. One man came to study theology under Witherspoon, but biblical principles of law of government were so

impressed upon him that he went on to become the chief architect of the United States Constitution and the fourth President of the United States -- James Madison. Witherspoon's training enabled him to accomplish this.
Witherspoon also trained:
- 1 vice president;
- 3 Supreme Court justices;
- 10 Cabinet members;
- 12 governors;
- 60 Congressmen (21 Senators and 39 Congressmen)
- Plus many members of the Constitutional Convention and many state congressmen.[4]

Pastors in Public Affairs

There is abundant evidence of the political/civil involvement of clergymen in Europe's history:
1. The clergy in the Roman empire who became judges
2. Patrick and his disciples who advised kings
3. Stephen Langton who drafted Magna Charta
4. Zwingli in Zurich
5. Calvin to the Geneva City Council
6. Knox to Queen Mary
7. Mornay in French government
8. Grotius in Holland
9. Kuyper in Holland

In America ministers participated directly in the public affairs of the nation:
1. They colonized and formed America's states. (Roger Williams - Rhode Island; Thomas Hooker - Connecticut; William Penn - Pennsylvania; Jason Lee - Oregon; Marcus Whitman - Washington).
2. They wrote America's laws and constitutions (e.g., Thomas Hooker - *The Fundamental Orders of Connecticut;* Nathaniel Ward - *Massachusetts Body of Liberties*).
3. They served as judges and lawyers, establishing and defending America's civil liberties.

4. They established schools to perpetuate their Biblical principles of liberty and they established universities to perpetuate their own order of an influential and learned clergy.
5. They also participated directly in civil government.

Samuel Davies, a pastor from Virginia, was typical of many pastors of the day as he went to extend the kingdom of God. He was involved in many things: Pastor, President of Princeton, a lawyer, an ambassador to England, Patrick Henry's friend and role model. While in England on matters of religious and civil liberty for his state of Virginia, an incident occurred which reveals his boldness. He was preaching where King George II and others in his court were in attendance. During the sermon, the King spoke several times to those around him and smiled. Davies paused a moment, and then looking sternly at the king, exclaimed, *"When the lion roars, the beasts of the forest all tremble; and when King Jesus speaks, the princes of earth should keep silence."*[5] The King kept silent during the rest of the sermon.

These and many other pastors were following the biblical example in their involvement in public affairs or politics. Clergymen in the Old Testament who became politically active were Samuel, Jeremiah, Ezekiel, Zechariah, and Ezra. In the New Testament, it was John the Baptist, Paul the Apostle, and Erastus. Politics is defined as "that which deals with the regulation and government of a nation or state, for the preservation of its safety, peace, and prosperity." God's leaders have always been involved with this -- they have addressed the direction of affairs of nations. The prophets of the Bible were simply statesmen and social reformers -- leaders of political movements in history. Samuel influenced Saul, Elijah influenced Ahab, Jeremiah influenced Josiah, John influenced Herod, and many more. Many of God's leaders actually held a public office (e.g., Joseph, Daniel, Esther and Mordecai, Moses, Samuel, and Erastus [see Acts 19:22; 2 Tim. 4:20; Rom. 16:23]).

What Then Should Be a Christian's View of the Separation of Church and State?

Establishing a Christian nation does not mean to set up an ecclesiastical state where the civil government leaders dictate how everyone is to believe and worship. A Christian nation is one that is established on Christian principles where God and His law is honored and obeyed. Within any Christian nation there will be a clear separation of church and state (but not God and government).

The idea of separation was first proposed by Jesus in Matthew 22:17-21. All pagan kings had claimed authority over religious matters, but Jesus proposed the world-changing concept that religion is under the authority of God and the church alone. Jesus proclaimed the idea of religious liberty or liberty of conscience.

Even in Old Testament Israel there was a division between the religious and government functions. John Eidsmoe writes:

> *"Israel was a theocracy recognizing God as its supreme ruler: all authority was derived from Him. But government functions were separated from religious functions; the kings came from the tribe of Judah while the priests came from the tribe of Levi. King Saul was severely punished when he tried to usurp the function of the priesthood by offering sacrifices himself -- his line was cut off from the kingship of Israel forever (I Sam. 13). When King Uzziah tried to burn incense on the holy altar, God smote him with leprosy, and he remained a leper the rest of his life (II Chron. 26:16-21). God seems to be telling the civil rulers in these passages, keep your hands off the church."* [6]

When Constantine made Christianity the official state religion of the Roman Empire around 312 A.D., religious tests were established for public officials - a national church was established. This ecclesiastical establishment brought great persecution during the Dark Ages until America's forefathers fled to America to practice their religious preferences free from a national state religion.

Almost every colony established a particular denomination as the official religion of that colony. But over time, dissenting Christian groups began to grow in many colonies. These dissenters began to experience the same persecution on the state level that their forefathers experienced on a national level in Europe.

After America won her independence, these dissenters began to work for disestablishment of preferred denominations in the various states. This was gradually accomplished over the years. Religious freedom was secured on the national level by the passage of the First Amendment to the United States Constitution. It states that, *"Congress shall make no law respecting an establishment of religion or prohibiting free exercise thereof...*" This does not mean as the courts have misinterpreted it in recent years, that the civil government of America is to be indifferent (and often hostile) toward Christianity and religion in general. It simply means that one sect of Christianity cannot be established as the national religion.

Every nation operates on the ideas and principles of some religion - be it Christian, Muslim, humanism, or whatever. A Christian nation, to remain free and prosperous, must operate on Christian principles. Every nation will eat of the fruit of the principles on which it operates.

Why The Influence of Christianity Has Eroded

The Father of American Geography, Dr. Jedidiah Morse, was a clergyman. He preached an insightful Election Sermon in 1799 from the Biblical text: *"If the foundations be destroyed, what can the righteous do?"* (Psalm 11:3). He said:

"To the kindly influence of Christianity we owe that degree of civil freedom, and political and social happiness which mankind now enjoys. In proportion as the genuine effects of Christianity are diminished in any nation, either through unbelief or the corruption of its doctrine, or the neglect of its institutions; in the same proportion will the people of that nation recede from the blessings of genuine freedom, and approximate the miseries of complete despotism. I hold this to be a truth confirmed by experience. If so, it follows, that all efforts made to destroy the foundations of our holy religion, ultimately tend to the subversion also of our political freedom and happiness. Whenever the pillars of Christianity shall be overthrown, our present republican forms of government, and all the blessings which flow from them, must fall with them."[7]

He said that the *"genuine effects of Christianity are diminished in any nation"* through (1) unbelief, (2) corruption of its doctrines, and (3) neglect of its institutions. Let us look briefly at each of these.

Unbelief

"And how shall they believe in Him whom they have not heard? And how shall they hear without a preacher?" (Romans 10:14).

123

"...The church of the living God, (is) the pillar and support of the truth." (1 Timothy 3:15).

Christianity cannot prevail in society without strong vibrant churches. These cannot exist without dedicated godly preachers. This by no means requires a majority of the population to be converted to be a godly nation. Throughout the American Revolution, only one third of the population were official members of a church (though many more attended). God never requires a "moral majority" to affect a nation only a "righteous remnant" who really understand their duties in all of life. The American Revolution (1760-1780) would never have occurred without the Great Awakening (1730-1750). Revival and awakening of the lost is, therefore, the remedy to unbelief.

Corruption of Doctrine

The doctrine that this refers to has nothing to do with your typical "statement of faith" that most Christians hold to as essential fundamentals. Those doctrines are generally confined to religious questions concerning the Godhead, salvation, etc.

The doctrines that, when corrupted or neglected results eventually in the decline of Christianity in society, were understood well by the apostles. These are articulated well in a sermon by Paul the apostle in Acts 17:24-28:

"The God who made the world and all things in it since he is Lord of heaven and earth does not dwell in temples made with hands; neither is He served by human hands, as though He needed anything, since He Himself gives to all life and breath and all things; and He made from one, every nation of mankind to live on all the face of the earth, having determined their appointed times, and the boundaries of their habitation that they should seek God, if perhaps they might grope for Him and find Him, though He is not far from each one of us; for in Him we live and move and exist."

Four primary doctrines that have practical implications on how we view the world are mentioned here:

(1) Creation - "God made the world."

It didn't just happen by chance. When this doctrine is not taught in a reasonable way, then Christians will began to neglect the field of science. Creation will become an irrelevant "religious" dogma. This neglect leaves a void for a competing ideology - Evolution.

Charles Darwin wrote his book in 1859, but it never really became predominant in public education until a lack of biblical scientific reasoning became the norm. Today, the tables are being turned, as Creation Scientists are restoring solid reasoning for Christians to articulate rather than simply saying, "the Lord made the earth."

(2) Lordship - "He is Lord of Heaven and earth."

This means He is absolute master and final authority to whom all must give allegiance. As this doctrine has been neglected, so another competing ideology has gained the ascendancy - humanism. Humanism says that man is the measure of all things and the one who determines right and wrong for himself.

(3) Providence - "He Himself gives to all life and breath and all things; ... for in Him we live and move and exist."

Truly God is the source of everyman's provisions, to Whom each man and woman must look. As this doctrine has been neglected, so the competing idealogy of socialism has prospered. The socialistic ideas promulgated in Karl Marx's book, written in 1844, will not have much influence where Christians live and preach biblical principles of economics. Also, a lack of Christian character tends to allow greed and materialism to grow and wealth to be accumulated instead of compassionately employed to meet the needs of the poor and society. Individual interests replace the common good of the community. These needs are then exploited by Marxist and Socialist leaders.

(4) Sovereignty - "He made... every nation... having determined their appointed times and the boundaries of their habitation."

When God's sovereignty is not taught in our schools, the ideology of existentialism will prevail. Existentialists believe history is meaningless and the future unpredictable and, therefore, to plan and work for goals is hopeless. Their philosophy is "Eat, drink, and be merry for tomorrow we die." It is totally present-oriented and hedonistic.

Liberating the Nations

Marshall Foster and Mary-Elaine Swanson warn that:

"Many Christians have subconsciously adopted the existential view of history. They de-emphasize their importance in a God-ordained historical chain of Christianity and see themselves simply as individuals God has plucked out of an evil world who are now just awaiting heaven. Their sense of responsibility for the past and their hope and planning for the building of the future are lost in the 'now generation' where they are called to focus on self-improvement. Until the Christian comes to grips with his historical duties, denouncing his existential perspective and reaffirming the providential view of history, the renewal of our nation will be impossible.''[8]

In colonial America and Reformation Europe *"the God of the Bible was seen as sovereign over men and their property.... But in the past 100 years a disarming doctrine, which sees Satan as the sovereign of this world, has been accepted by many in Christian circles. Many bible teachers today see Jesus as an absentee king who is concerned exclusively with building and maintaining His church until He returns to earth. They see Jesus as having the authority and right to rule, but as having given over powers to subjugate the world temporarily to Satan.''* The world-view of the reformers was diametrically opposite to this view. They saw Jesus Christ as the ruler of the earth (1 Timothy 6:16; Hebrews 2:14) and Satan as a defeated foe (John 12:3, Colossians 2:15).

"One's attitude toward the sovereignty issue is of paramount importance, because it affects what is done in every area of life.

"If you see God ruling the earth:

"1. Your commission is to subdue the earth and build godly nations through evangelizing and discipleship.

"2. You see Christian culture as leavening all areas of life, replenishing the earth, and blessing all mankind.

"3. All of God's world is His and every activity, to be seen as a spiritual work of God.

"4. Reformation is expected if a nation is obedient to God's word.

"If you see Satan ruling the earth:

126

"1. Your commission is just to concentrate on saving souls from this evil world.

"2. You see Christian culture as a counter-culture, an isolated, persecuted minority in an evil world.

"3. Church activity is primary and spiritual, while worldly pursuits are secular and to be dealt with only as a necessity.

"4. Reformation is impossible since things must get worse because Satan is in control."

"The above contrasts illustrate the importance of ideas in determining consequences, because to the degree Christians have abdicated their leadership role and denied the 'crown rights of Jesus Christ,' to that degree the humanists have filled the void."[9]

What is the remedy for the corruption and neglect of these vital doctrines? It is the restoration of biblical Christianity and its teaching of practical theology, and biblical reasoning in all areas of life.

Neglect of Institutions

If the church in a society neglects the educational, economic, social, and political institutions, then those people who lack Christian character and thinking will begin to assume control of these areas. As these institutions are operated upon a worldly philosophy, they will cease to provide liberty and justice for all, and will cause the nation at large to decline.

The remedy for the neglect of institutions is the **reformation of all society.** As Christians commit themselves to be the *"salt of the earth,"* corruption will subside, *"the righteous will be in authority,"* and *"the people will rejoice"* (Proverbs 29:2). *"Righteousness exalts a nation"* (Pr. 14:34).

Summary of Action Steps

Churches must begin once again to provide a regular program of discipleship for their members, either through a weekly class for adults or through home groups or special study groups that are set up for this purpose in the congregation. Near election times or around special community events and national holidays, special sermons should also be preached. These election and commemorative sermons can be preached on Sundays at church or at special seminars for the general community. Distributing these sermons in printed form will help disseminate the truth.

In addition to this, the church should try to help supplement the schooling efforts of parents by starting private schools or by coordinating special tutoring and events for home-schooling parents. Clergy should also be seeking to develop relationships with community leaders in the government, business, and media spheres so as to provide consultation and advice from a biblical perspective.

Chapter 10

The Arts, Media, & the Press

The Bible and the Arts and Media

There are of course no references in the Bible to the means of communication that are available today such as television, motion pictures, radio, stereo, or newspapers. But the Bible does address the subject of the media in terms of the means of communication at the time. By studying this we can deduce certain principles that apply to any form communication may take.

The Bible speaks of communication in the form of oral history, drawings, sculpture, drama, dance, poetry, prose, music, writing on scrolls and parchments, parables and stories, preaching, etc. The Bible shows the people of God using all of these forms of communication at various times. It also shows pagans using some of these forms for their own ungodly purposes.

We cannot deduce from the Scriptures whether each form of communication began by God inspiring one of His people to invent it or whether some pagan originated it. Historically we know that sculpture, drama, and music have been used since the most primitive of times. Ancient Egypt developed the use of elaborate pictures (Hieroglyphics) as early as 3300 B.C. and China did so around 1800 B.C. The alphabet was developed by the Semites and Phoenicians around 1600 B.C. The Egyptians developed papyrus for writing on around 1000 B.C and just prior to the Christian era they developed parchments. Paper was invented by T'sai Lun in China around 100 B.C., yet it was not used in Europe until around 800 A.D.

Although pagans invented many of the forms of media in ancient history, the Hebrews and Christians always had the approach that those things were in themselves but tools that could be used for good or for evil - there was nothing inherently wrong with any form of communication. Christianity for most of its history has always taken things of this world that were not manifestly sinful and stripped them of their pagan associations and ennobled them with godly content. Christians up until this last century had an orientation toward life that said all things were spiritual and sacred. The idea of secular or worldly things was unheard of until the 20th century. Christians saw themselves as called to be involved in all aspects of the world as salt and light, not as some counter-culture group that needed to keep itself separate from those things that weren't specifically religious or church related.

For this reason, the people of God have historically excelled in the arts and other forms of communication. The poetry and prose of the Bible is unequalled. The musical culture of the Hebrews starting with David was prolific. The dramatic sermons of the prophets, which were acted out using many props, were very effective at catching the attention of the masses and conveying an important message. Hall and Wood write in *The Book of Life* of this effective use of the media by the prophets:

> "...*The prophets themselves used dramatic representations to enforce their great messages. Jeremiah went to the potter and got an earthen bottle. Then he called the elders of the people together in the valley of Hinnom. Holding the bottle in his hand, he preached a short and very effective sermon on the sins of the city. Then he threw the bottle down and broke it into fragments. After he had broken it, he said, 'Thus saith the Lord of Hosts, "Even so will I break the people and the city as one breaketh a potter's vessel, which cannot be made whole again"' This was a most telling dramatization of Jeremiah's sermon. When the elders went home and thought it over, they would see that bottle broken in fragments and the remembrance of it would help them to remember the words of the preacher...*
>
> *"The prophet Ezekiel made a little model of Jerusalem in clay. Then he added the camp with the forts and mounds and battering rams of a besieging army. Then he took an iron pan and placed it between himself and the city. This was a dramatization of the way in which the city would be sieged...*
>
> *"The Passover was a vivid dramatic representation of the escape from bondage, enacted with great impressiveness in every home down to the present day. Part of the significance of the Lord's Supper lies in its dramatic representation of the sacrificial love of Jesus for his disciples, a memorial of his death 'until he comes.' "*[1]

Prior to the development of writing, the oral story of the Gospel was preserved by star-pictures (i.e. the constellations of the Zodiac) so that the ancient Patriarchs could enhance their communication by pointing up at the stars. These constellations are mentioned in the earliest book of the Bible, Job. God used the stars to communicate His promises to Abraham. It was these constellations that guided the three Magi (astronomers) to the city of Bethlehem to find the Messiah. Jesus was a master at story-telling and the use of parables in order to communicate important truth to the masses. The Apostle Paul not only preached the Gospel orally as did other Apostles but also made use of "parchments" (2 Tim. 4:13) available at that time as a means of communication.

The Media and Arts in the Christian Era

The Christians put great value on communication via letters and written Gospels and preserved them over the early centuries of Christianity. Hall and Wood write of some of the contributions Christianity made in the advancement of various arts:

"When the age of martyrdom was over and Christianity began to build its own churches, often upon the ruins of pagan temples, a new form of art came into being. The people were still ignorant and unlettered. How better could Bible stories be taught to the people than by picturing them upon the walls of the places of worship? These early pictures were of mosaic. They are called 'Byzantine' because they originated in Byzantium, the old Constantinople...

"After this period Europe was overrun by the barbarians of the North, and almost everything which was precious and beautiful was destroyed.

"Then came the forming of the great monastic establishments, and Christian art was saved by the monks, who themselves practiced, and taught the people, not only the practical arts -- agriculture, metal-working, building; -- but also the fine arts and crafts. However much monastic life may have degenerated later, the world owes to the monks of this period all its possessions of knowledge, saved from the utter wreck of the barbarian invasion. 'Pictures are the books of the ignorant,' said Augustine. It was necessary to teach the Bible to people who had no books, who could not have read them if they had had them. So the Bible stories began to appear again upon the

131

walls of the churches in pictures and sculpture, crude at first but gradually growing more beautiful...

"Then came the great building age all over Europe, lasting for nearly four hundred years, when the wonderful Gothic cathedrals were built, -- such glorious buildings as those of Amiens, Chartres, Rheims, in France; Lincoln and Durham in England; Burgos in Spain. It was a time of great religious fervor. Everywhere over Europe churches were built, not only the great cathedrals but churches in every town and village...The cathedral of Chartres...and its adornments {the windows and sculptures) tell the Bible history in stone... These great buildings were built and the Bible was illustrated so completely in the carvings of the great western portals that Ruskin called that of Amiens, 'The Bible of Amiens.' Every important incident of Bible history is portrayed... While these sculptures are crude, still they are very vigorous and expressive, and there was no more effective way of teaching the Bible to the people of that time...

"In Italy there began to be felt the need of a finer way of teaching the Bible than by sculpture, and out of this desire came the development of pictorial art. The earliest period, which is called 'The Gothic period,' was from about 1250 to 1400. Among the earliest painters were Cimabue and Giotto. The paintings were upon the walls of churches in fresco, and the subjects were practically all Biblical..."Then came the periods of the early Renaissance, 1400-1500, and the later Renaissance, 1500-1600. To these periods belong the mighty masters; Raphael, Leonardo da Vinci, Correggio, Michael Angelo...It must be borne in mind that this great development of art, the greatest the world has ever seen, was called out by the Church and was devoted to the church in its efforts to teach the Bible to the people. Many of these paintings are in galleries now, but originally they were painted for the walls and altars of churches."[2]

The Canon of Scripture was completed in the first few centuries A.D. and by medieval times monasteries were organized and devoted to the meticulous copying of the Scriptures by hand on paper. While the Bible was being preserved it was largely hidden from the common man. Ignorance of the Truth resulted in a stagnant period in history, known as the Dark Ages, with little advancement in most areas of life. History shows that the introduction of the Bible in a society results in the advancement of all fields of life, including the arts, music, and communication. When John Wycliffe translated the Bible into the common English of 1382, he was providing the seed for the great change and advancement that would take place in every area of life in the following centuries.

In 1455 it is estimated there were 50,000 books total world-wide. In that year Johann Guttenberg invented the printing press in Germany. Ten years later the total number of books had increased to 10 million. It is easy to see why the printing press was a major breakthrough in communication. Due to the importance of its content, the first book printed on the press was the Bible.

The distribution of the Bible to the masses caused Europe to arise out of the "dark ages", and was the reason the arts began to flourish as never before in such fields as paintings, sculpture, classical music, poetry, and prose. While non-Christians were involved in such media, by far most of the greatest contributors to the arts were Christians who felt called of God to glorify Him through that avenue.

The Dutch school of Art produced men like Rembrandt - the foremost painter of Bible subjects. Leader of the Protestant Reformation, Martin Luther, took a popular tavern song and turned it into one of today's best loved Church hymns - *"A Mighty Fortress Is Our God"*. English clergyman, Isaac Watts, compiled a hymnal that was used widely for many years. In the beginning of the 18th century two of the greatest classical composers of all time, Johann Sebastian Bach of Germany, the master of church music, and George Frederick Handel, famous for composing the *"Messiah"*, set the early example of using Scriptural themes for their music. Charles Wesley and the Methodists contributed greatly to the communication of truth through the medium of hymns.

The first newspaper in the world was started in China around 1000 A.D.; the first in Europe was begun in 1615 in Germany and known as the *"Frankfurter Zeitung"*. America's first newspaper was *"Public Occurrences"* established in 1690 in Boston. However, the main source of news in America for over 200 years came from the clergy through regular sermons on Sunday, as well as special weekday "political" sermons or lectures. This has been replaced today by the television news anchor man. News now is reported from a pagan worldview rather than a Biblical one.

Another development in communication in America was the establishment of a postal system between towns. This network made it possible for the American colonies to unite in political philosophy and strategy through dispersion of papers and letters generated by the Committees of Correspondence, which were started by Christian statesman Samuel Adams. These letters were a unique use of the media by the Christian social reformers of the American Christian Revolution.

How the Bible in the Hand of the Individual Produced Freedom of the Press

J. Lee Grady, Assistant Editor of National and International Report, writes:

"It is in the pages of Scripture that the idea of freedom of the press was introduced to the world. When the prophet Nathan stood before King David, pointed his finger at the most important ruler in the nation of Israel, and said *"You are the man!"* -- he dramatically demonstrated that all men are subjects of the God of Heaven and are accountable for their evil deeds. Nathan's pointing finger is an excellent example of the role of journalism -- it plays a prophetic role in society, exposing darkness and reminding rulers that they cannot trample on the commandments of God.

"This is why the gospel of Christ shook the Roman Empire to its foundations. The entire First Century world was gripped by the pagan idea of man. Emperors held absolute sway over the lives of their subjects and were revered as gods. Yet Christ stood before Pilate and announced to him that Rome's authority was not absolute:

"You would have no power over me if it were not given to you from above."
(John 19:11)

"The idea that earthly thrones and authorities are subject to God's rule was a foreign concept to the world at that time, yet within a few centuries this truth had conquered the known world. The seed of the gospel continued to leaven Europe as Christ's message spread. When the Bible finally became available to the common man, more and more courageous prophets spoke out and challenged the established political and religious systems of the day. Olasky points out that it was John Foxe who is credited with being the first English-language journalist because he pointed his finger at the sins of the Catholic Church and recorded the abuses of popes and priests in his *Foxe's Book of Martyrs* -- the first example of eyewitness reporting.

"England was stubbornly resistant to the concept of freedom of the press. The British Crown suppressed all published dissent on the principle that this would secure peace and public safety. The Christian poet John Milton, however, made an early appeal for freedom of the press in his famous *Aereopagitica,* published in 1644. He summarized a truly Christian idea when he wrote

". . . though all the winds of doctrine were let loose to play upon the earth, so truth be in the field, we do injuriously by licensing and prohibiting to misdoubt her strength. Let her [truth] and falsehood grapple; who ever knew truth put to the worse, in a free and open encounter?"

"This idea was penned centuries earlier by the author of Proverbs, who described Truth as a woman broadcasting her message in the public square while Folly lures her victims into a deadly trap. Truth and Falsehood are depicted as competing in the open market of ideas.

"Ministers in America helped to promote this "free and open" climate for free speech and a free press. In an election sermon delivered in Boston in 1795, Perez Fobes stated forthrightly the biblical basis for the journalist's right and duty to expose wickedness:

"Rulers are ministers ordained of God only when they are the ministers of good to the people. Obedience therefore, to civil rulers imposed on the people, or to any form or administration of government contrary to the will of the people, was never inculcated by the inspired Apostle [Paul] on pain of damnation: for the same authority which in this instance condemns, in others justifies open resistance and opposition to government. The unreasonable humor of King Ahab of Israel, the menacing edicts of Nebuchadnezzar, and the peremptory edict of the Egyptian Monarch were disregarded with impunity, and even without blame. Was it a crime in Hushai to develop the machinations of Ahitophel? Or did Mordecai speak evil of dignities when he exposed the plot of Haman against the whole nation of the Jews?... Should the highest officer of any government on earth flagrantly abuse the authority of his station, even by prosecuting private designs, or by adopting public measures hostile to the public good, it is not a crime, but the duty of a free people to be free enough to speak evil of him. The tongue in this case is the proper weapon, where the laws of men cannot reach. This will keep the public mind awake, by adding stimulus to ardour and information."[3]

Counter-Cultural Christianity

With the explosion of so many new forms of communication in the 20th century, Christianity should have the easiest time of any period in history to be the salt and light of the world. This means not just evangelism and communicating about "religious" subjects, but influencing the entire culture in every sphere of life by educating in a Biblical worldview.

Unfortunately, the 20th century has instead proven to be the greatest period of apostasy and secularization of American culture. Pagan philosophy has become dominant in the television, radio, music and movie industry. And the sad thing is that this has not happened because paganism conquered Christian thought. Rather it has happened simply because Christians began to accept a faulty theological premise in the late 1800s that taught them to separate from the things that were "worldly" or non-spiritual and that it was useless anyway to waste your time in such things because things were going to get worse and worse before the end-time return of Christ. Thus, although it happened very slowly, by the 1960's virtually every influence of Christianity on the media had disappeared and pagan world-views and philosophies were allowed to gain the ascendancy by default. Now Christians see themselves largely as an irrelevant counter-culture and thus the world sees them that way as well.

Ted Baehr of Good News Communications and author of the syndicated *Movieguide* writes:

"...From 1933 to 1966, the Church influenced communication flowing from Hollywood. For 33 years, scripts were read by representatives of the Roman Catholic Church, the Southern Baptist Church and by the Protestant Film Office. During that period, there was no sex, violence, profanity, or blasphemy in movies. Also, films could not mock a minister of religion or a person's faith. For the most part, movies and television programs communicated the true, the good and the beautiful.

"In 1933, the Hollywood studios and producers, under pressure from organized religious leaders, agreed to follow the Motion Picture Code, which stated:

1) No film or episode may ridicule any religious faith.

The Arts, Media, & the Press

2) Ministers of religion should not be portrayed as comic characters or as villains.
3) Religious ceremonies should be carefully and respectfully handled."

"The code exercised considerable influence over the content of motion pictures until the mid-'60s, when the Roman Catholic Legion of Decency, the Protestant Film Office and the Southern Baptist Film Office stopped approving Hollywood scripts and issuing 'seals of approval.' The Legion of Decency changed (from)...approving Hollywood scripts...to rating films. The Southern Baptist Film Office...retreated completely from the Hollywood landscape. The Protestant Film Office, taken over by the liberal National Council of Churches, abandoned its role. In its vacuum came the Motion Picture Association of America rating system (G,PG,R and X) in 1968, but in reality, the Motion Picture Code was abolished. The equivalent to the Code in the Television industry was the NAB Code and it was dropped in 1988, although the network's in-house censors had stopped upholding it many years ago anyway.

Today you will find in PG and PG-13 movies, the ones many parents think are acceptable for children, the following:

* *25% have the "f-word"*
* *61% take the Lord's name in vain*
* *71% contain vulgar references to excretion, intercourse or the genitals*
* *50% imply sexual intercourse*
* *13% show intercourse*
* *30% feature explicit nudity*
* *75% display moderate or severe violence*
* *74% depict alcohol and/or other drug abuse*

"Now scripts are read by homosexuals, feminists and Marxists, but not by Christians. These groups award pictures and television programs which communicate their point of view and condemn movies and television programs which disagree with their point of view. For instance, one television network had to spend hundreds of thousands of dollars to re-shoot and re-edit a television movie so that it wouldn't offend the Alliance of Gay and Lesbian Artists."[A]

137

A Strategy for Reformation of the Media

Christians have been diligent to claim every new form of media communication for evangelistic purposes and have done quite well at it. They also have a significant lobby through the National Religious Broadcasters Association. But most Christian programming takes place rarely in primetime; most is found in the "religious" time slots on Sunday mornings. Few have worked to invest their time into using media to communicate in a comprehensive way. Few Christians have worked at going into the major newspapers and magazines and television networks and Hollywood with the goal of bringing a Biblical worldview to bear upon it. If Christians have gone into these fields it's been largely for personal career reasons - very few having a goal beyond perhaps witnessing for Christ to their associates. There have been successful films recently with Christian themes (for example, *Chariots of Fire*), yet these have not been the product of the Christian community.

The same is true of music, drama and dance. The Christians have their "religious" music, etc. which witnesses for Christ but few are infiltrating or buying out the mainstream companies for such art. In the world of painting and sculpture, Christians are constantly complaining about the filth that is funded by the National Endowment for the Arts and displayed in art museums all across the country. Christians with a solid Biblical worldview need to become the directors of such museums and government agencies, but when have you last heard of a teenager in one of your evangelical or charismatic churches talk of such a career? Such things are too worldly for them or just unimportant compared to religious goals.

In recent years Regent University has begun to train its graduates for such careers, and this is a refreshing beginning. And the Christian Broadcasting Network is trying more and more to become a comprehensive type of "Family Channel". Terry Wild of California has a plan for a national newspaper like "USA Today" that would be based on a Biblical worldview. Billy Graham's Worldwide Pictures has done an admirable job at film-making yet most of these are not reaching the masses because they are known to be evangelistic films.

In addition to making films and starting newspapers that are designed largely for Christians, we must also provide resources in the arts and media that will impact all men with a Biblical worldview. As Augustine might say today: "Television, movies, and videos are the books of the ignorant."

138

Christians must utilize this source of the arts to communicate a comprehensive view of life that is Christian to the hundreds of millions of ignorant men in the world today.

Christian businessmen need to be investing and buying out the major television networks and motion picture studios and theatre chains across the country. They need to be buying out the major newspapers like the Moonies did with the *Washington Times* a few years back. They need to be buying out the major music studios and record companies. They need to reestablish a Hollywood film office and motion picture code that is godly. Good News Communications is working toward this and has established an office in Hollywood already. It is important that we are there being a watchdog of what trash pagans produce, but why should we expect them to produce anything else? Christians need to go beyond that and become the producers themselves and not just the reviewers.

The idea of spending so much money on such things seems to be hard to rationalize, especially when Christian media-ministers tell you that you should spend it instead on funding their shows.

But until we once again see that this is true spirituality and that it is essential for redeeming our culture, it will never happen. We will still go on as the largest voting block in America, yet complaining in our living rooms that our side, the pro-life, pro-family, pro-morality majority never gets fair coverage in the news or decent programs on prime-time. The media will continue to control the elections, the public opinion, the framing of the debates of the issues of our day.

In *A Time for Anger*, Franky Schaeffer says:

"It is time for those who are Christian to reassert themselves in the arts. And it is time for the Christian community to back them. We must fill people's imaginations with the images of the Christian vision. The arts and media must be a focal point for protest against the pagan world that has come upon us, while we have had our Christian heads in the sand of 'spirituality.' " [5]

Jesus and the prophets were the master story-tellers of their time. The media is simply a story-telling tool. We need to imitate our Lord and once again take up the weapons of our warfare which are ..."*mighty in God for pulling down strongholds, casting down arguments and every high thing that exalts itself against the knowledge of God, bringing every thought into captivity to the obedience of Christ..."*(2 Cor. 10:3-5).

Lee Grady writes:

[W]here there is freedom of religion, speech, and the press, the gospel can spread openly, unhindered. It was here in the United States that ground-breaking communications technology was invented and developed: radio, television, telephones, and satellite systems. These tools have now made even the most tyrannical nations vulnerable to the principles of the gospel and made them accountable to public scrutiny. The seed of Christ's message, carried via the airwaves, or by video cassette, or by short wave radio, now penetrates even the most closed nations of the world. And everywhere the seed is planted, the Christian idea of man and government takes root. It happened in America. It is happening today in Moscow and Bucharest and Prague. It will most assuredly happen in Beijing and Baghdad and Teheran.[6]

Chapter 11

The Framework of Godly Government

The Cry for Democracy

In the past few years millions of Eastern Europeans, Russians, Chinese, and other peoples have demonstrated and cried out for freedom. They equate freedom and democracy and think democracy is necessary to correct the problems in their nations. But many people do not really know what democracy is or what makes it work. There are certain principles that can be derived from the Bible, and also from attempts at democracy in world history, that we must learn or else suffer from the awful mistakes that others have already experienced in trying to establish a free government. [These principles were examined in Chapter 1.]

The cry for democracy is common to many countries in the world today. Millions of people from every race and culture recognize the need for reformation of their society. Almost half of the world's population (2.1 billion people) live in poverty. Five hundred million live on the edge of starvation. One hundred and ten countries have been documented as violating basic human rights even to the point of torture. The number of people killed by their own totalitarian governments in the 20th century exceeds the number killed by war by almost four to one. The annual number of refugees in the world is about twenty-eight million. Added to these grim statistics are international terrorism, debt, crime, the threat of nuclear war, and escalating military coups.

141

In the face of such world problems there is a movement all over the world toward democracy. On every continent there are multitudes saying that this is their desire. However, the term *democracy* has different meanings to different people, and therefore needs definition and explanation.

Many people simply associate the concepts of freedom and democracy as the same. But, in reality, freedom is what democracy exists to protect. Protection of individual rights and liberties is the goal, but democracy is the means. Certain rights are recognized by all people as inalienable - that is, they can never be denied to anyone without injustice. Such rights as freedom of religion, freedom of speech, freedom of assembly, freedom of the press, freedom of petition, and freedom of self-defense are of this nature. All inalienable rights can be summarized in three categories: the right to life, the right to liberty, and the right to property. All human beings recognize that to kill, steal, or oppress another person is wrong, whether it is done by an individual or by governmental force.

The famous American President, Abraham Lincoln said that, *"We all declare for liberty; but in using the same word we do not mean the same thing;...The shepherd drives the wolf from the sheep's throat, for which the sheep thanks the shepherd as his liberator, while the wolf denounces him for the same act;...Plainly, the sheep and the wolf are not agreed upon the definition of liberty."* Lincoln said that some believe liberty means, *"that each individual in the society may do as he sees fit with himself and the earnings from his labors."* While others believe..."*That some persons may do as they see fit with other person's labors."*

True liberty is not unbridled license. Government must provide a system of justice to address grievances while protecting the inalienable rights of individuals in the society. Therefore, the same authority structure that governs the people must also restrain the government itself.

Democracy literally means rule by the people. World history shows that when people rule their nation, their rights are safer than when governed by one man or a few men. Centralized power in the hands of a few can be corrupted very easily. But it is also true that power in the hands of **many** people can also be corrupted.

Pure democracy as attempted by Greece in ancient history and France 200 years ago proved to be not only impractical but also dangerous. Where people rule directly they tend to favor the will of the majority at the expense of individual rights of minorities. Tyranny, therefore, can be found in pure democracy. It can become "mob rule" and endures only until threatened minorities finally join together against the majority using force to protect themselves. The result is chaos and anarchy such as seen in the "reign of terror" in France after their revolution. The result of this is that order is usually restored only by a totalitarian government, as occured in France with Napoleon Bonaparte. This cycle was repeated in Greek and Roman attempts at democracy.

The father of the Constitution of the United States, James Madison, noted that democracies "...*had been spectacles of turbulence and contention...incompatible with personal security or the rights of property.*"

Pure democracy, therefore, is to be avoided. How? By the concepts of representation and fixed higher law, which are associated with the term "republic." A Biblical form of government may better be termed a representative democratic republic or a constitutional democracy. Henceforth, these elements should be kept in mind when we use the general term "democracy." To say "democratic republic" or "representative democracy" or "constitutional republic" would be better.

We need to define the practical aspects of democracy even further if we want to avoid the mistakes of other democracy movements of history. Following are seven basic governmental structures that are found in the Bible and are necessary to protect and secure individual rights and liberties. These comprise the essential framework of a Godly government.

The Framework of a Constitutional Republic

Decentralization of Government - Federalism

We saw in Chapter 3 that the pagan tendency is always to centralize power. This began with the building of the tower of Babel in Genesis 11 which God condemned.

Since power residing in the people is a basic premise of democratic government, the government should be kept as close to the people as possible. This can be accomplished by establishing a small national government and strong local and regional governments. The Hebrew Republic had a government that was a decentralized, family-based system. It had local town and tribal (regional) governments that were independent of the national government. They were known as the elders of the cities who met in the gates (Exod 24:1; Num 11:16,17).

Such a division of powers will be a safeguard against the tyranny of centralization since it will allow the people to most fully participate in government and to keep watch over the flow of power through the governing officials. (For example, in 1 Kings 12:1-16, had Rehoboam listened to the people and his counselors, the nation of Israel may not have split.)

History has shown that centralization of governmental power destroys the liberty and the rights of man. The way to have good and safe government is to divide the power among the people and the localities, instead of entrusting it to one body.

Civil government in a country should be subdivided into many levels (local, regional, national). The power of each level should be clearly defined and sovereign in those defined areas. No level of government should be able to usurp the jurisdiction of another. A great majority of the power should rest on the local level.

The limited powers of the national government should be clearly defined in a constitution, and involve those things which affect the country as a whole, such as defense, foreign policy, regulation of interregional and foreign commerce, citizenship laws, coining money, and copyrights. All other powers should remain with the people, or with the local, and regional governments. The powers of local and regional government can be written in a regional constitution and include such things as traffic regulations, business regulations, public works, voting procedures, and law and order.

Jesus Christ taught the principle of limited government and sphere sovereignty in Matthew 22:36-40. He said that "Caesar" may only do certain defined things, and that the other institutions, such as the church and the family, have their defined responsibilities and, therefore, sovereign rights of jurisdiction. This is true also between national and local governments.

Constitutionalism

The concept of constitutionalism began with the Hebrew Republic when Moses presented the Book of the Covenant to the people at Mount Sinai. It contained the Decalogue and the companion body of law. Contrary to impressions that one may have of this as being an arbitrary top-down imposition of law, the reality is that, although the laws were written by God, they were read and submitted to the people for adoption. The people had to agree to live by them before they would be of benefit (Exodus 19:5-8; 20:2-17). This initiated the concept of a national covenant or constitution which must be agreed upon by the people before the government has legitimacy.

Later on, when Israel had a king, he had to enter into a covenant with the people where he promised to govern according to the Book of the Law, which was their constitution (1 Chron. 11:3; Deut. 17:14-20). For David, it mattered not that he was already anointed by a prophet of the Lord; he had to enter into a covenant with the people's representatives as well. This idea is articulated well in the United States Declaration of Independence which says that "just powers are derived from the consent of the governed".

This concept is part of the idea of Federalism because it comes from the Latin word "Foedus" meaning covenant. In a decentralized government a written constitution or contract will enable the people to be able to see if the national government oversteps its authority. This usurpation of power can be resisted by the local and regional governments rallying together.

In a decentralized government a constitution, and not the national ruling party, is supreme. It should only be amended with the consent of the people and the local and regional governments.

A government of liberty will be a government of laws, not of rulers or of the majority. In a pure democracy, a simple majority (just over 50%) of the people rule. The rights of the minority could be in jeopardy under such a government. Therefore, the best form of democracy will be a constitutional democracy. Here, the law is supreme, and protects the rights of all people.

Throughout most of history people have been governed by laws imposed by their rulers. In this they had no choice. In a democracy the people will form their own constitution and consent to it. Hence, they establish a government of people's law, not of ruler's law. Both the people and the rulers are subject to the law. This is essential for protecting the individual's rights to life, liberty, and property. Citizens must not only be protected from harmful acts of other citizens, but also from abuses by their own government. Since the law is supreme and not the rulers, the people will be protected from ruler's tyranny.

145

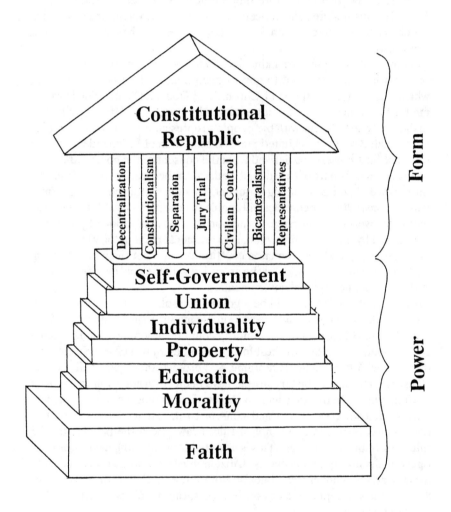

The Power and Form of a Free Government

A constitution will define and limit the power of government. It acts as a chain to bind down rulers from misusing power. It is written so that it will not be forgotten.

Any government is free to the people under it, no matter what structure it has, where the laws rule, and the people are a party to those laws. Any government opposed to this will be one of tyranny.

A constitution formed by the people should not deny the rights of others. The laws will apply to all people equally, regardless of political position, religion, race, wealth, social status, or creed. Everyone is equal before the law in relation to protection of their life, liberty, and acquisition of property.

A parliamentary form of government is one in which the supreme source of law is the Parliament rather than a fixed higher written constitution. Parliament then tends to favor whatever groups gain the majority coalition and potentially may oppress the rights of minorties and individuals as it pleases. Any approach to rights based on ethnic or special group rights is ultimately dangerous to the rights of those groups or individuals out of favor with the government in power. Geographic representation is Biblical, but ethnic or tribal representation is not (unless all of a tribe or ethnic group is within a specific geopraphical area and no one else lives there)(Exod 24:1; Num 11:16,17).

Separation of Powers

A difficulty in forming any government where men are over men is that you must first enable the government to control the governed and then insure that the government controls itself. Men tend to abuse power, especially if they are given too much. It has been said that all power tends to corrupt; absolute power corrupts absolutely. Due to this tendency of abuse, power must be limited in our civil rulers.

We have seen that prescribing specific powers in a constitution is one way to accomplish this. Another way is to separate governmental powers into different branches with different personnel running each branch. Every government (whether a monarchy, oligarchy, democracy, etc.) exercises these three functions: legislative - lawmaking, executive - enforcing and carrying out laws, and judicial - interpreting laws.

In the Hebrew Republic there was a recognition of these three functions in Isaiah 33:22. It said that "The Lord is our King, the Lord is our Lawgiver, the Lord is our Judge". God being perfect and all wise can exercise all functions righteously, but sinful, finite men cannot.

There should be a division of functions and personnel between the legislative, executive, and judicial departments. It is setting up three separate branches with prescribed separate functions (in a constitution), where no person should serve in any two branches at the same time. This serves as an internal control of abuse of governmental power. Since men are not angels and tend to lack self-control, separation of powers will guard against tyranny.

The French political writer, Montesquieu, wrote in *The Spirit of Laws* (1748):

> *"When the legislative and executive powers are united in the same person, or in the same body of magistrates, there can be no liberty; because apprehensions may arise, lest the same monarch or senate should enact tyrannical laws, to execute them in a tyrannical manner. Again, there is no liberty, if the judiciary power be not separated from the legislative and executive. Were it joined with the legislative, the life and liberty of the subject would be exposed to arbitrary control; for the judge would be then the legislator. Were it joined to the executive power, the judge might behave with violence and oppression."* [1]

Tyranny will result when legislative, executive, and judicial powers are all accumulated in the same hands, of one, a few, or many. This is also true of all rulers, whether hereditary, self-appointed, or even elected. Simply giving power to the people and allowing them to elect their leaders is not an assurance of securing liberty for all. One thousand despots would be as oppressive as one. We do not want to establish an elective despotism. Separating governmental powers into three branches is one of many controls on the government needed to keep the people's rights and liberties from being endangered.

The three branches should be independent of each other with no one branch having total control of another. As an example, the legislative branch should not be able to remove the executive or judiciary very easily; and the executive should not be able to dissolve the legislative or judiciary. While independent, these branches should not be completely separate, but should band together through a system of checks and balances. This will permit each branch to guard against one department encroaching into another, which would result in tyranny.

An example of checks and balances is the executive having the right to veto laws passed by the legislature, and the legislature being able to override the veto with a larger percentage vote by their members.

A well-defined system of checks and balances will help maintain the separation of powers in three branches. While a separation of powers will produce some conflict between the branches of government, this will assist in preserving the three branches of government and the system of checks and balances. To preserve them is as necessary as to institute them.

Independent Judiciary and Trial By Jury

Another check on sinful men abusing their governmental powers is having a court system with judges independent of the executive or legislaive branch, and by having trials by jury. In a nation under law, any violation of the law requires a judge. Wrongdoers must be punished and required to make restitution to deter crime, yet, there must be an orderly process of justice where the guilty and innocent are distinguished. Judges should not only be knowledgeable of the law, but also honest, refuse bribes, and not show favoritism.

The Hebrew Republic emphasized an independent and impartial judiciary (2 Chr 19:5-10; Exod 23:1-3; Deut 17:6; Lev 20). It also asserted in passages such as Deut 19:15-19 that (1) One is innocent until proven guilty, (2) there is a right to due process of law, (3) One cannot be forced to testify against oneself, (4) Accusers must be personally present to confront you so they may be cross-examined, and (5) the right to appeal to a higher court(Deut 1:19).

History is replete with examples of judges manipulated by government authorities to further their political agenda. An independent judiciary is essential to ensure that the written boundaries established by a constitution are maintained. The judicial system should be made up of un-elected individuals who will not be swayed by political pressures. The courts are the ones who keep an eye on the legislative and executive branches of government and determine their faithfulness to constitutional standards.

Individual judges, even if un-elected, may at times be manipulated by other government leaders to render unjust decisions, against political opponents of the government. Therefore, in order to protect individual liberty, and guarantee a fair trial, there needs to be a judicial system that uses a jury drawn at random from society. These jury members should generally be on the same social level as the defendant. They also should be from the same city or geographical area as the defendant, yet should not know any facts about the case in advance that might color their perspective. The jury must be protected against government reprisals themselves in order to be independent. A jury of peers should be effective because it can judge of the defendant's character and the credibility of the witnesses.

There is freedom in a society that guarantees that neither life, liberty nor property can be taken from the possessor, until a dozen or so of his countrymen shall pass their sentence upon oath against him. Government becomes arbitrary without such a system of justice. The legislature could pass oppressive laws or a judge could deliberately misinterpret the law.

The jury system was foreshadowed in the Hebrew Republic(Deut 19:15-21) and in the teaching of Jesus concerning taking cases to the people(Matt 18:15-17). It was fully developed in British law over 1000 years ago. Governments, whether fascist or communist, have forbidden trial by jury. The United States, in contrast, conducts about 120,000 jury trials each year.

Civilian Police and Militia

Another crucial curb on the power of sinful men in government is a civilian-dominated and controlled police and militia. The Hebrew Republic clearly separated the leadership of the army from the Executive branch; Moses was the Executive and Joshua was the Commander of the military; David was the king and Joab was the commander of the military. These commanders would have authority over a small peacetime professional army such as David had in his 600 man bodyguard and forces for use in emergencies until the militia could be gathered (1 Sam 23:13). These commanders would lead the overall military strategy of the militia when they were called out in times of war, but the militia divisions had their own locally elected officers (Deut 20:9; Num 31:14). The members of the militia supplied their own weapons which presupposed the right to bear arms (1 Sam 25:13; Num 31:3; 32:20). Any attempt to prohibit the right of an individual to own arms was unbiblical and is a pagan attempt to centralize power (Judges 5:8; 1 Sam 13:19-22). The leaders of the local militia could refuse to serve if they judged that a war was unjust that their nation was waging (2 Sam 20:1; 1 Kgs 12:16).

Military and police power is a necessity in society to protect citizens from criminals and enemies, both foreign and domestic. A wise and prudent people will always have a watchful and jealous eye over this power. The American statesman, Thomas Jefferson, said that "the supremacy of the civil over the military authority" is an "essential principal" of democracy. His draft of the Declaration of Independence condemned the British King for rendering "the Military independent of and superior to the Civil" authorities, and also for keeping "standing Armies without the consent of our people."

World history has proven repeatedly that armies that are supposedly the "people's," - i.e. there to protect the people's interests as a whole, are in reality being used by powerful government leaders to further their goals. Many nations experience military coups regularly and the generals of the armies run the nation rather than "presidents" and "constitutions."

In order to ensure civilian control of the military, a constitution could establish an elected head of state ("president") as the commander-in-chief of the armed forces in war time. However, rules for the military should be established by elected representatives of the people other than the head of state. These elected representatives should not be able to spend money for armies for more than the period of time until they face re-election. This keeps the support of the military power by the representatives subject to the approval of the people.

The officers of the armies should not be appointed by the head-of-state, but by elected representatives from their own geographical area. The majority of a nation's army should simply be working citizens who have their own weapons and can be called together quickly. By doing this, no permanent army can exist that can be taken control of by a political leader. This system allows any citizen to own his own weapon, which will give everyone the ability to defend himself, and will also give a geographic area of people the ability to defend themselves from armies that do become pawns of the government.

The police force should be locally and regionally controlled and completely separate from military power. The head of the police forces should be elected and governed by local government. The rest of the police should be hired by the government as normal employment.

Election of Representatives

Another crucial part of the framework of free government is the election of representatives. Although those governmental powers and offices are severely limited and checked, the men who are to fill those positions must be elected by the people and forced to face those same people frequently in order to be re-elected. This establishes accountability.

Half of the national legislature of the Hebrew Republic was composed of an elected house of officers called "judges" which were selected on the basis of population, not regional or tribal representation (Deut 1:13-17; Exod 18:21-26). Another house in their legislature was composed of two appointed "elders" and two scribes/lawyers representing each geographic region (tribe) plus the 24 priests totaling 70 men. This unelected body was known as the Sanhedrin. The elected representatives of the people however were chosen on the basis of population: 10s, 50s, 100s, and 1000s. Moses would swear them in or "appoint" them only after they were selected by the people (Deut 1:13).

Frequent elections are essential, but also it is vital that the elections be free. This means that those who run for office can do so without restriction of being from one party. One party may possibly dominate elections but it must come through winning the battle in the free marketplace of ideas. The right of any citizen to form a party and offer candidates for election is essential.

The vote in a nation must not be compulsory if it is to be free. It must be voluntary, plus it must be available to all citizens equally, regardless of race, color, social status, religion or gender. The vote must also be by secret ballot so that no pressure nor fear of reprisal can influence the outcome.

Once the election determines the winner there must be a commitment to the peaceful transition and relinquishing of power by the previous office-holders. It is essential also that all competing candidates and parties work to be unified for the common good of the nation.

It is important, however, that not all government offices be filled by popular choice. In order to prevent the politicalization of the judiciary, for example, it would be best that judges remain appointed by elected representatives.

Another safety necessary to prevent majority tyranny and ensure more healthy gradual change in a nation would be for different portions of the legislative and executive branches, on both the national and regional levels, to be up for elections on different years. This would prevent radical changes from taking place without time for the electorate to fully weigh the potential consequences.

Bicameral Legislature

A bicameral national legislature is one where the responsibilities for making law is divided among two groups or "houses". One reason for dividing it is to create a check or safeguard, so that before a law goes into effect it must pass the vote of two houses, and then be approved by the chief executive. This structure is based upon the Biblical view of man, who being sinful tends to abuse power. Thomas Jefferson said: *"What has destroyed the liberty and the rights of man in every government which has ever existed under the sun? The generalizing and concentrating all cares and powers into one body.... The way to have good and safe government is not to trust it all to one, but to divide it..."*

In creating two houses in the legislature there should be a clear delegation of authority concerning which laws orginate in each body. For example, one house could have the exclusive power to make laws dealing with taxing and spending and the second body could simply have the power to veto it. The second house could make laws dealing with war, defense, and foreign affairs, while the first house would have veto power over it.

In determining how the two houses are constituted, the Bible shows that it should be done in a way that one house represents regions or states and the other house represents individuals in a numerical population. The first house should not be elected by popular vote but rather by the state or regional legislatures so that the interests of those areas as a whole would be strongly represented and deter centralization of power. State or regional legislatures will know how to best pick a representative who will be knowledgeable and qualified to work for their state's or region's concerns.

The other house, however, needs to be organized so that its representatives are elected by the people directly to speak on their behalf on various issues. It is this body, which is directly answerable to the people, that should be given the most power over the purse - the power to tax and spend.

This type of government was established in the early Hebrew Republic. There was one group of leaders elected by the people based upon population. It began when Jethro, the priest of Midian, advised Moses on improving the government in Exodus chapter eighteen. Moses recounted it in

Deuteronomy 1:13-15. He commanded the people to *"Choose wise, under-standing, and knowledgeable men from among your tribes, and I will make them heads over you...leaders of thousands, leaders of hundreds, leaders of fifties, leaders of tens, and officers for your tribes."* They were known as "judges" or "officers". (The term "judges" was also used for positions in the judicial and executive branches of government.)

These "officers" were a different group of representatives than those unelected leaders of the various clans and tribes known as "the elders" that Jethro and Moses first explained the above plan to in Exodus 18:12. These elders were seventy in number (Exodus 24:1 and Numbers 11:16,17). The "Seventy" later became known as the Sanhedrin. (Over the centuries the sanhedrin was changed to include not just elders but also priests and scribes, although this was not the original plan.)

This model of government was incorporated by the United States of America in its original Constitution, with the Senate selected by the state legislatures and the House of Representatives elected directly by the people in districts determined by population. In 1913, however, an amendment to the Constitution made the Senate an elected body directly selected by popular vote, which was a step away from the Biblical model.

These seven structures of government, based upon biblical ideas and biblical models, will provide safeguards for the protection of individuals' God-given rights to life, liberty, and property. We should remember that the purpose of civil government is to protect law abiding citizens and punish criminals. It has no jurisdiction over the mind and the soul. Therefore, government should be prohibited from interfering with the church, the press, the school, and the marketplace. The American Constitution did this when it said: *"Congress shall make no law respecting an establishment of religion, or prohibiting the free exercise thereof; or abridging the freedom of speech, or of the press..."*

Though it is important to establish these biblical structures of government, it is more important for the citizens of a nation to continually work to place godly men in office who can establish justice even without an ideal form of government. It must be remembered, as William Penn wrote in his *Frame of Government for Pennsylvania* in 1682, that *"though good laws do well, good men do better."*

154

Chapter 12

Principles of Christian Economics

Defining Christian Economics

Since economics is the science that deals with production, distribution, and consumption of goods and services, Christian Economics is the "discipline that studies the application of Biblical principles or laws to the production, distribution, and consumption of goods and services." It entails "how men use God-given natural resources, ideas, and energy to meet their human needs and glorify Him."[1]

A Christian Economy will Flow from the Heart of Man Outward

Christianity produces internal liberty in man, which is the foundation for a Christian economy. The internal change of heart that Christ brings produces Christian character and self-government which is necessary for an economy to be prosperous. Christian character and self-government produce:

- People who will not steal. Billions of dollars are lost each year by American businesses to theft by their employees. This theft is much greater than that by non-employees.
- People with a strong work ethic who will labor hard and be productive. This will cause an economy to grow.

155

- People who will save and invest to acquire greater return later.
- People who have concern for their posterity and will seek to pass on a greater estate than they received.

The truth of the gospel also imparts new ideas and creativity to man which assists him in increasing his material welfare. This occurs as man creates new and better tools. In addition, man gains the understanding that God has given him an abundance to rule the earth and if he seeks His supply, he will find it.

Besides bringing internal liberty to man, the introduction of Christianity in a nation will also manifest itself externally in political freedom. A government acting on Biblical principles is needed for a Christian economy. As Verna Hall stated, "government is the house in which the economy lives." Its policies must promote and protect economic freedom.

Economic freedom will then flow from personal and governmental freedom. Charles Wolfe states that this freedom includes "a people's freedom to own their own property...to choose their own occupation...to keep the fruits of their labors...to buy and sell in a free market, where wages and prices are determined not by government mandate but by voluntary exchanges of free men and women."

Factors of Production in a Society

Stated in a simple manner, man's material welfare is a product of natural resources mixed with human energy and coupled with the use of tools. Mr. Wolfe represents this by the following formula:

N.R. + H.E. x T. = M.M.W.

Natural Resources + Human Energy x Tools = Man's Material Welfare

If *Natural Resources* increase, so does *Man's Material Welfare*. If *Human Energy* is exerted, *Man's Material Welfare* increases. If better tools are created, *Man's Material Welfare* will also increase.

This equation for *Man's Material Welfare* is applicable for every nation in the world, yet there is a great difference in how men in a Christian society view the world and apply their physical and mental energies as compared to those men in a secular society. We will examine the factors of production in both a Christian and secular society.

In a Christian Society with Great Economic Freedom

Natural Resources

God created man and knew that he would have certain basic needs, such as food, clothing, and shelter. God created everything that was needed to meet those needs. One, God created natural resources. Those men with a Christian worldview believe that God has provided all that they need and, consequently, they have faith to seek, find, and process abundant natural resources. As the Natural Resources available to man increase, his material welfare increases as well.

Human Energy

God not only created natural resources, but He also created man with human energy. God told him to "have dominion" or rule over the earth (Genesis 1:26). Man was placed in the garden to cultivate and keep it (Genesis 2:15), which required labor. After the fall, cultivating the ground required an additional "sweat of [man's] face" (Gen. 3:19).

In a Christian society, men will be inspired by God to work. In addition, in a nation of economic freedom, men will be able to partake of the fruit of their labors which will encourage them to exert more energy. As man works harder and exerts more human energy, his material welfare (and that of the nation) will increase.

Tools

From the beginning, man was unable to cultivate the ground and rule over the earth, or even meet his basic needs well, with his bare hands alone. Mr. Wolfe writes that "to take the natural resources God (had) created and turn them into... food, clothing, and shelter" to meet man's needs, tools were needed to help him "till the soil, to cut down trees and saw timber, to mine and refine minerals, and to tend sheep and weave wool." Knowing this, God gave man "ideas for inventing and making tools." Man was given "intelligence and physical strength," that is "mental and muscular energy," to take the Natural Resources and create tools to meet his needs.

Man has used tools from the beginning. Adam and Cain were farmers and likely used simple tools (possibly a digging stick or simple plow) and some kind of sickle or cutting tool to harvest grain. Abel was a shepherd and likely had a rod and staff.

The Bible has many references to tools. Wolfe states these include "hammers, axes,...plows drawn by oxen, millstones for grinding meal,...furnaces for refining silver and gold, ovens, and baking and frying pans."

Wolfe writes: "The usefulness of each tool is measured by the amount of time and energy it saves; by the increase in the quantity and (or) quality of the goods and services that can be produced through its use."

The following chart reveals how advancements in agricultural tools have produced economic progress (remember that tools are a multiplying factor in the equation of man's material welfare):

Time Period	Tool	Production by one man
Adam	Simple Tools	Probably enough food for Eve and himself
Abraham	Wooden Plow drawn by oxen	Food for large family
18th Century	Horse drawn iron plow	Food for 3 families
1940's	Tractor	Food for 14 families
Today	Advanced tractors and tools	Food for 60 families

Development of better tools has primarily occurred in nations where people have had access to the truth of the Bible (and hence the mind of Christ) which has enabled them to receive many ideas for inventing new and better tools. As we have seen, these advancements in tools have caused man's material welfare to improve.

We should remember that man's productivity is a result, not only of better, but also of better use of those tools. That is why we must be diligent in our work. God has given man all he needs for his human welfare -- natural resources, human energy, and ideas for creating tools -- but man must labor to take what God has given and transform it into the food, clothing, shelter, and other things that meet his human needs. Labor is the title deed to property.

In a Secular Society with Limited Economic Freedom

The factors of production in the equation, N.R. + H.E. × T. = M.M.W., are viewed differently in a secular society by those with a nonchristian world-view, than those in a Christian society.

Natural Resources

A secular society will lack faith in God's providence and, consequently, men will find fewer natural resources. The secular or socialist has a limited resource mentality and views the world as a pie (there is only so much) that needs to be cut up so that everyone can get a piece. In contrast, the Christian knows that the potential in God is unlimited and that there is no shortage of resources in God's earth. The resources are waiting to be tapped.

We do not live in a resource-short world. Known reserves of minerals and energy resources are greater today than in 1950 despite increasing consumption. Ideas allowing us to tap into unused natural resources are limitless. For example, about 100 years ago, the American Indians wiped oil on their faces. Today, new uses of that natural resource have transformed our economy and brought a higher standard of living for everyone. In recent years, the computer world has been revolutionized by the silicon chip, which is made from the same material as sand.

While many secularists view the world as over-populated, Christians know that God has made the earth sufficiently large, with plenty of resources to accommodate all the people He knew would come into existence. There is plenty of room and food for the entire world population today. All the five billion people on the earth could live in the state of Texas in single family homes with front and back yards and be fed by production in the rest of the United States. Present world agricultural areas, if developed by present technology, could feed 31 billion people. Our earth has plenty of room and plenty of natural resources.

Human Energy

Those with a secular world-view will lack a God-inspired strength and work ethic. Such strength and character would cause them to be more productive through hard labor, honesty, investment in the future, etc. In addition, the lack of incentives of freedom found in secular nations with limited economic freedom cause men to exert less energy since they cannot eat of the fruit of their labor. The net result is that man's material welfare suffers.

Tools

Secularists are cut off from the Bible and the mind of Christ (the chief source of creativity), and so they get fewer ideas for inventing new and better tools. Lack of new and better tools keeps production and man's material welfare from increasing.

Comparing the factors of production in Christian and secular societies reveals why some countries prosper and some do not. Mr. Wolfe writes: "While men and women in every country try to multiply their human energies with the help of tools in order to transform natural resources into useful goods and services, Christian free societies generally do it more efficiently than others."

A study by Dr. Browning of incomes of different nations and people groups confirms this observation. He found that "between protestant and catholic groups it was noted consistently that the protestant countries had higher per capita income than the catholic countries. But those that were not Christian had no income or low incomes or were starving to death."[2]

There are a few exceptions to this finding. The most notable is the nation of Japan. However, the reason that Japan has prospered is that "they have simply imitated the principles and techniques on which America's original prosperity was built" -- principles that grew out of our Christian society (and which have in part been abandoned today).

As Mr. Wolfe reveals, the Japanese have imitated America's Puritan work ethic, Yankee ingenuity, the idea that "a penny saved is a penny earned," individual responsibility for quality of work, giving workers a voice in the decision making process of businesses, and encouraging workers and managers to come together in a kind of voluntary union.

While application of these principles have caused the material welfare of the Japanese to increase greatly, this increase has come at the expense of greater life and liberty in other areas. Material welfare is not the only aspect of a Christian economy. The pressure to succeed is so great upon many Japanese youth today, that many are not holding up under the stress. Many are also "sold out" to their jobs and work so much they have no time for anything else.

In a Christian economy people will earn more with less work which means:

- People will have more free time for worship of God, instruction, recreation, and service to others.
- People will have more money to give to Churches, charities, and foreign missionary efforts.
- People can acquire more luxuries.

The Real Wealth of a Nation

While America has in recent years abandoned some of the principles that produced our prosperity, she is still the most prosperous nation in the world. Wolfe writes that "the best way to compare the real wealth of the people of one country with the wealth of the people of another is how many hours of work it takes a factory worker to earn the money needed to buy the same basic commodities in retail stores in that country."

To purchase a kilogram of bread, a factory worker must work 18 minutes in Moscow, 12 minutes in London, and 8 minutes in Washington. To purchase a car (Volga, Ford), that work time is 35 months in Moscow, 8.5 months in London, and 4.1 months in Washington.

If you visit the Philippines, you will find that clothes are 1/3 to 1/4 the price of those in the United States. While this may be of benefit to the American traveler, this price reflects a much greater percentage of the average Filipino income than Americans spend on clothes. An American worker's average income is about 10 times that of the average worker in Manila. So the average Filipino spends more of his income on clothes and food than the average American, even though these items are less expensive in Manila than the United States. Filipinos spend much more on other items because appliances, cars, and other things not made in the Philippines, cost more than they do in the States.

Why Are Some Nations in Poverty?

As we have seen, the equation, N.R. + H.E. × T. = M.M.W., applies to every country in the world. Those societies built on Christian principles will have a proper view of natural resources, the character to exert human energy, and access to the creativity of God leading to better tools, all of which cause man's material welfare to increase. While any nation adhering to this truth will see the material welfare of it's citizens increase, most people and nations are quite poor. In fact, 46% of the world lives in poverty today. Why? Some claim that it is because many nations lack natural resources. Yet, some nations, such as Japan, with few natural resources are quite prosperous. There are also many nations with abundant natural resources that are much less prosperous than other nations with fewer natural resources.

The primary reason that nations are in poverty is lack of spiritual resources and truth. A secularist world-view keeps each element of the factors of production from increasing, which stifles man's material welfare. India is a good example of how a people's religion directly affects it's economic prosperity. Today, India has widespread hunger problems, yet these are not due to a lack of food, but are a result of the people's religious beliefs. The majority of Indians are Hindus. The Hindu religion teaches that people who die are reincarnated as animals; therefore, their laws and religion prohibit the people from killing rats, mice, cows, or other animals.

There are 200 million "sacred cows" in India. Each cow eats enough food to feed seven people. The feed from these cows alone would feed 1.4 billion people, which is over 1/4 the world's population. The mice and rats, which they will not kill, eat much of their grain as well. This grain, not to mention the meat from the cows, would supply plenty of food for all the starving people of India.[3]

The economic state of a nation depends upon its religion.

Profit Motive

We have seen that man's material welfare increases in a Christian Society because Christian faith and character help "enlarge, vitalize, and improve" the three factors of production. But, as Charles Wolfe writes:

162

"The economic incentives of freedom are also important. To find and process natural resources such as oil and minerals is extremely costly. So is the protracted process of researching, developing and producing new and more efficient power tools. The profit motive provides individuals with the needed incentive in a Christian free economy based on individual enterprise."

"History shows that in a Christian free economy. . .men tend to invent more and better tools, invest more in producing those tools, and use those tools more efficiently than in a secular society with limited economic freedom."

In recent years many nations that have operated on communistic economic principles, which eliminate the profit motive, have been allowing more individual enterprise because it causes the people to be much more productive.

Communal farming with no individual incentive does not even work with Christians who have common vision, goals, and purposes. The Pilgrims gave us this example in their first two years in America. Compelled by the contract with their financial backers, the Pilgrims farmed the land communally. The lack of incentive to work resulted in such a poor crop that the Pilgrims almost starved during the first two winters. To alleviate this problem, the leaders shifted to an individual enterprise system where every family farmed their own parcel of land, and ate the fruit of their own labor. Governor Bradford wrote that "this had very good success; for it made all hands very industrious. . .The women now went willingly into the field, and took their little ones with them to set corn, which before would aledge weakness, and inability; whom to have compelled would have been thought great tyranny and oppression." They produced an abundant crop and never lacked for food again. Their example shows that "the taking away of property, and bringing in community into a common wealth,"[4] does not make people happy or cause them to flourish, as many ancients, such as Plato, or modern men, such as Marx, have espoused.

The Wheel of Progress in a Christian Economy

The diagram of the "Wheel of Progress in a Christian Economy," (see next page) as given by Charles Wolfe, is an excellent depiction of the necessary elements of a growing and prospering economy. We will look at the individual parts of the wheel.

The Hub of God-Given Liberty

We saw earlier how a Christian Economy revolves around or flows out of the heart on man -- from the internal liberty that Christ brings. This God-given liberty, which begins internally but is manifested externally, is the hub of the wheel of progress in a Christian economy.

It is important to recognize that this liberty or freedom is granted by God and not by man or the state. Mr. Wolfe writes that "if the hub of the wheel is seen as freedom granted by man or the state, rather than by God Himself,

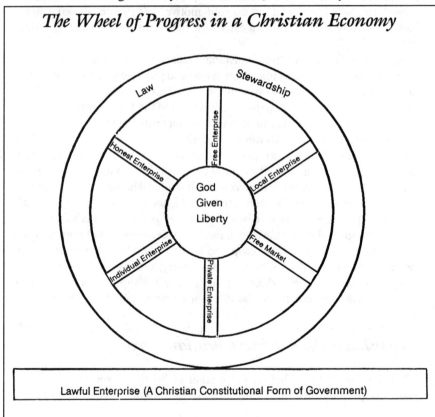

The Wheel of Progress in a Christian Economy

Stewardship

Law

Free Enterprise

Honest Enterprise

Local Enterprise

God Given Liberty

Individual Enterprise

Free Market

Private Enterprise

Lawful Enterprise (A Christian Constitutional Form of Government)

then that freedom can readily be taken away, in whole or in part, and there is no reliable basis for a continuing, consistent free economy."

The hub, seen as God-given liberty, has a reliable core "to which the various spokes -- the Biblical principles of economics -- can be securely attached." In fact, only a hub of God-given liberty can give rise to the various spokes, for it is only in an economy of liberty that men are allowed to practice individual enterprise, economic self-government, and manifest each aspect of the spokes.

Rim of Stewardship and Law

The spokes in the wheel of progress in a Christian Economy will be held together, and the wheel will run smoothly, by the discipline of God's law and the practice of Christian stewardship. These make up a rim of responsibility which keep economic freedom under God's control.

In an economy -- as in all society -- the great challenge is not merely to maintain freedom, but to maintain freedom with order. To do this, people must be disciplined from within so they do not infringe upon the rights of others. Therefore, men must understand and obey God's law in order to have a Christian economy, for as they do, the following will result:

● Men will respect each other's property.

In many nations today, people must have a half dozen locks on their cars, and walls, fences, and guards protecting their houses and business to keep other citizens from stealing their property. Growth of the economy will be hindered greatly in this environment.

● They will not steal or cheat one another.

A recent visitor to the United States from another country was amazed at many things he witnessed in this country. One thing that he especially took note of were newspaper stands. He marveled that people would put in a quarter and take only one newspaper. He said that this would never happen in his country, because the first person to get their in the morning would put in his quarter, take all the newspapers, and go and sell them on the street. This is a small example of how dishonesty hinders economic freedom. We mentioned before how businesses in the U.S. lose more money by theft from their employees than outside forces. For a nation's economy to grow, the people must be honest.

● They will abide by contracts.

- When citizens are elected or appointed to positions in government, they will not use their power to secretly erode the value of the people's money through inflation, nor will they gradually restrict the people's economic freedom through excessive regulation.

A Christian businessman in a developing country needed to get some raw materials through customs so that he could fill large orders for various customers. Before these materials could be released he needed to get 46 different signatures of government officials. Most of these officials wanted a bribe before they gave their signature, and when the businessman refused, there was such a delay in getting his materials released that he was unable to fill his orders in time, and he lost hundreds of thousands of dollars. Excessive regulation and dishonesty stifle economic growth.

To maintain economic freedom, individuals must also practice Christian stewardship. Wolfe says that they must:

- Be industrious in earning money
- Be disciplined in saving money
- Be wise in investing money
- Be obedient to God's law in how they share it with their church and with those in need
- Practice "the self-denial necessary to restrain themselves from buying many things that would bring immediate gratification, in order to save and invest enough to provide for emergencies and their later years, without having to turn to government for assistance."

In other words, people must work all they can, earn all they can, save all they can, and give all they can.

The Title Deed to Property is Labor.

John Locke writes:

"Though the Earth, and all inferior Creatures be common to all Men, yet every Man has a Property in his own Person: This no Body has any right to but himself. The Labour of his Body, and the Work of his Hands, we may say, are properly his. Whatsoever then he removes out of the State that Nature hath provided, and left in it, he hath mixed his Labour with, and

166

joyned to it something that is his own, and thereby makes it his Property. It being by him removed from the Common State Nature hath placed it in, it hath by this Labour something annexed to it, that excludes the common Right of other Men.[5]

All property you possess was acquired by labor--either your labor or someone else's. You take possession or title to property in proportion to your labor or individual enterprise. This is not only true of external property but also internal property.

Rosalie Slater writes:

"We might use the example of learning of a subject in school as an illustration of this principle which Locke is setting forth. God has given the knowledge contained in this subject to all of us--you might say it's our common possession. Yet no one actually has title to it--can prove that he owns it. If any student makes the effort to learn the subject--he acquires title to what he learns. This effort on his part hasn't in the least diminished the amount of the subject which we all still have in common. It's still there. But the student who made the effort to learn the subject does have a title to something which no-one can take from him and which he would not have had if he had not added or invested his own effort. He has property rights in the subject."[6]

The Measure of Property

If through labor people acquire more property, what is to be the measure of how much one accumulates? John Locke tells us that the measure of property is not how much one wants, but how much one needs--that is what is sufficient for an individual to fulfill God's will in his life.

The Title to Internal Property is Obtained by Consent.

Miss Slater explains this idea well:

"Just as the Christian values the talents which God has placed in trust with him, and just as he works for their productive fruition in our Lord's service, so he carefully guards the use and disposal of his property. Today much concern is expressed about 'property rights' and the infringement upon individual or private enterprise. But the first invasion of property rights occurs internally when the individual consents to the disposal or use or mis-use of

his opinions, his religious convictions, and his faculties. Often this consent is tacit consent. John Locke differentiated between express consent and tacit consent. The word tacit means:

"Tacit: 'Silent; implied, but not expressed. Tacit consent is consent by silence, or by making no objection.

"'So we say, a tacit agreement or covenant of men to live under a particular government, when no objection or opposition is made; a tacit surrender of a part of our natural rights.'

"Thus the surrender of an individual or a nation can occur by silence, or by making no objection. Christianity, unlike any other religion, requires an active confession of faith, an active acceptance of Jesus Christ as Lord and Saviour. So a Christian also must refuse, through whatever duly constituted means are at his disposal, to permit his rights of conscience, his convictions, or, indeed, his very faculties, and talents, to be used contrary to what he knows to be good and true, and in accord with the laws of God. Consent is one's title to the property of conscience. And as John Locke reminds us only express consent makes one a "member of any Commonwealth". So only express refusal to have one's property used for purposes which do not support righteous government can make one truly faithful to the stewardship of conscience."[7]

The Spokes

1. Individual Enterprise

The idea of individual enterprise, which we spoke of before, follows from God's Principle of Individuality. Every person on earth is distinct, unique, and important in an economic sense. It follows that:

* Each person has "special God-given talents as a producer." This leads to specialization and division of labor (which leads to greater wealth in a nation).
* Each person has "individual desires as a customer."
* Each person has "individual rights, such as the right to enter an occupation of one's choice" (which promotes greater productivity), "the right to start one's own business, and the right to buy the goods one prefers."
* Each person has "individual economic responsibilities." Each citizen should provide for themselves and their family rather than rely upon the

civil government to meet their needs. They should also voluntarily help the poor and those with genuine need. According to the Bible, providing for the poor is the responsibility of individuals and the church. The state has assumed this responsibility in countries where the church and individuals have given it up.

Caring for the Poor

Welfare states are not biblical and do not work. America in recent decades has shown this to be true. While government money spent on welfare has increased dramatically, so has the nation's poverty. Today, only 30 cents of each welfare dollar actually goes to meet the need of the poor. The other 70 cents is consumed by the governmental bureaucracy. Since President Johnson announced his war on poverty in the 1960's, America has spent hundreds of billions of dollars on the fight, yet poverty is increasing. Government money is not the solution to poverty. Compare the following figures:

- In 1950, 1 in 12 Americans lived below the poverty line.
- In 1951, government spent about $4 billion on social welfare programs.
- In 1979, 1 in 9 Americans lived below the poverty line.
- In 1981, government spent $316.6 billion on social welfare programs. [8]

The Bible says that the family and church are the primary institutions of health, education, and welfare. As we reassume our responsibilities, we can eliminate the need for the civil government to spend hundreds of billions of dollars on welfare.

Individual enterprise opposes economic collectivism and its emphasis upon the group and forced common production. Individual enterprise applies the Bible Principle, "as you sow, so shall you also reap," which encourages productivity.

2. Economic Self-Government (Free Enterprise)

An individual who governs himself will direct and control his own economic affairs in a responsible manner. He will be:

* "A self-governed producer" -- "not needing constant supervision...to assure the quality and quantity of his work."

* "A self-governed customer" -- "buying only what he needs and never spending in excess of his income."
* "A self-governed saver" -- "regularly saving some of his earnings to assure a strong economic future."
* "A self-governed manufacturer or retailer" -- "producing and selling quality goods and services, with due concern for the rights and needs of employees and customers."

A nation of self-governed people will cause the economy to grow and remain free.

3. Christian Character (Honest Enterprise)

We have already seen how Christian character is the foundation for a free and prosperous society. A few specific character qualities that effect the economy of a nation include:

* Diligence and industry -- hard work increases productivity which brings about increased prosperity.
* Faith in God's Providence -- hard work alone does not guarantee prosperity; we must also trust and obey the Lord to experience His blessings (Matthew 6:33; Deuteronomy 28). Individuals and the nation must put their faith in God to experience His blessings.
* Love for our neighbor -- As we express Christian love, we will care for the needy in the land.
* Honesty -- Honest employees will not steal from their employers; an honest civil government will not steal from its citizens by use of fiat money.

4. Private Property (Private Enterprise)

The Principle of Property was examined in Chapter 1 and in Chapter 11. We saw that property is first internal and that private property rights are a basic necessity for any society that desires to be free and prosperous. Noah Webster wrote:

> "*The liberty of the press, trial by jury, the Habeas Corpus writ, even Magna Charta itself, though justly deemed the palladia of freedom, are all inferior considerations, when compared with a general distribution of real property among every class of people...Let the people have property and they will have*

power -- a power that will forever be exerted to prevent a restriction of the press, and abolition of trial by jury, or the abridgement of any other privilege."[9]

A Christian nation will "let the people have property" and hence power.

5. Local Business (Local Enterprise)

Economic growth occurs as small businesses (that may grow into large businesses) are started locally by responsible individuals who have prepared themselves -- people who do not depend on someone else to employ them, but who save their money, get an idea for serving others, become self-employed, win customers, and then employ others. This is how new jobs are created. This is how our economy grows.

Christian education will produce such knowledgeable and motivated individuals in our nation. These people will not look to the government to create jobs but will be entrepreneurs and assume that responsibility themselves.

6. Voluntary Union (Free Market)

A voluntary working together of all peoples and regions of a nation will encourage economic growth. This would prohibit any tariff barriers within a nation and create a nationwide "common market." This would allow each person in each region or district of a nation to do what he could do best (and working with the natural resources in his locality), and exchange it for the production of others, using honest money as the medium of exchange. Each person is free to sell or not to sell at whatever price they want to offer, but they cannot force anyone to buy. Exchange of goods and services is voluntary and will occur as all involved believe they benefit from the exchange.

The prices of goods and services will be determined by "supply and demand." In a free market the supply of goods and services will balance out the demand for those goods and services at a price buyers are willing to buy and sellers are willing to sell. The greater the supply of any particular kind of good or service, the more the price will tend to go down. The greater the demand for any kind of good or service, the more the price will tend to go up.

171

The Road Bed: A Christian Constitutional Form of Government (Constitutional/Lawful Enterprise)

A civil government built on Biblical principles provides the road on which the wheel of economic progress can turn with great efficiency. Such a government, rooted in the Law and the Gospel and based on the Christian idea of man and government will assist economic progress by providing an environment of freedom with order in which production and exchange can flourish, protecting private property, punishing theft and fraud, and not providing for the people's economic needs.

Such a government will be "limited in its functions and cost -- to have just enough power to guard the citizen's rights, but not the power to interfere with honest economic activities."

Taxation

> *"Render unto Caesar the things that are Caesar's and unto God the things that are God's."*

Civil governments need money to accomplish their responsibilities of providing defense, punishing evildoers, and keeping the peace, Gary DeMar writes:

> *"In the United States the Constitution is our 'Caesar.' We are bound to pay what it stipulates is our due. But, neither citizens nor civil representatives must assume that Jesus gave rulers a blank check in the area of taxation...Paul informs citizens to pay taxes due to civil authorities (Romans 13:7). Notice that Paul does not say 'What they want.' The state must limit taxing authority to those areas specified by God's word."* [10]

A progressive income tax is a nonbiblical means of taxation that destroys personal property rights. These oppressive forms of taxation have come upon our nation as we have refused to govern and provide for ourselves as God intended us to. When Israel stopped wanting to be self-governed and asked for a king to rule over them, they got a king with greater centralization of power. One consequence of this was the confiscation of their property through taxes (see 1 Samuel 8).

Types of Taxes

1. **Income tax** - "Another word for taxes is tribute. If God requires only 10% (tithe), to give civil government more would indicate the giving of greater allegiance. This is idolatry." [11]

2. **Property tax** - "Civil government in the United States, in direct violation of biblical law, owns all the land in the country, and rents some of it to its citizens. If you do not pay the property tax (rent), you will be evicted. This is theft: The government has no right whatsoever to tax property, and the principle of eminent domain is a claim to deity. It is specifically forbidden in Scripture (I Sam. 8:14; I Kings 21; Ezk. 46:18)." [12]

3. **Inheritance taxes** - "Nowhere does the Bible allow the fruit of a man's labor to be taken from him after he dies and before his children receive it. This is one way that the kingdom is continued and built. Godly children should not have to start at the bottom when they begin. This increases the wealth in the kingdom of God." [13]

In a Christian economy the children will be wealthier than their parents because the estate will continue to grow and be built up with each generation.

Biblical Taxes

The Bible mentions two kinds of taxes:

1. **Head Tax or Poll Tax (Ex. 30:11-16)** -- This tax supported the state in its duties. It was an uniform tax that each male over 20 paid. It was of necessity small so the poor would not be oppressed in paying it.

2. **Tithe** -- A tenth of each person's increase was given to the priests and Levites for them to meet the necessary ecclesiastical and social functions of society. It supports the church and aspects of welfare, education, and other godly social needs. We could say the tithe is a "tax" on people's income. If citizens would tithe, the amount of money the civil government would need to collect would be drastically less.

Honest Money

A biblical economy will have an honest money system. Leviticus 19:35-37 states:

"You shall do no wrong in judgment, in measurement of weight, or capacity. You shall have just balances, just weights, a just ephah, and a just hin: I am the Lord your God, who brought you out from the land of Egypt. You shall thus observe all My statutes, and all My ordinances, and do them: I am the Lord."

Money is a commodity. It is something of genuine value in the marketplace, whether cattle, coconuts, shells, silver or gold -- all of which have been used as money. Historically, exchange began with barter. Money makes exchange much easier, because people can trade their goods for money and use the money to buy other things they want. In the Bible money was silver or gold, a precious metal. This is money based on principle.

"Paper money initially is not money. It is a substitute for money, and is useful because it is difficult to fold coins into a wallet. But if paper money is honest, it will always be backed by a specific amount of real, 'hard' money and redeemable at any time."[14]

America was on a gold standard throughout most of her history. In 1933 she shifted to a silver standard. In 1968 her silver certificates were replaced with Federal Reserve Notes thus eliminating honest money from the nation. When America had honest money there was never any prolonged inflation in the nation. Today's paper money is not backed by anything except the government's promise that it is good. Compared to a 1932 dollar, the U.S. dollar today is worth about 5 cents. It is interesting to note that an ounce of gold today will purchase about the same amount of goods that an ounce of gold bought 60 years ago.

Money with no precious metal backing, fiat money, allows the central government to spend more than it collects in taxes, because it can print new "money" (increase the money supply) anytime there is a need. This is inflationary.

Inflation

Greg Anthony writes that *"one of the Biblical signs of a nation backsliding is the condition of its currency and the degree of honesty in its weights and measures. When nations began backsliding in history, dross (common-based metal) began to appear in their coinage."*[15] In rebuking Israel from turning from God, Isaiah points out how *"your silver has become dross"* (Isa. 1:22).

To many people today, inflation means an increase in prices. This, however, is simply the symptom of the national government increasing the money supply to pay for their budget deficits. When the money supply is increased, either through printing more money or credit-expansion, the purchasing power of each dollar falls, and businesses must increase the prices they charge to keep up with their own higher costs.

Anthony says, *"the only one to benefit from inflation is the first one to spend money, (i.e. the government). It is a hidden form of tyrannical taxation because as the government spends more and more money created from thin air, the purchasing power of the citizen's bank account goes down and down. Inflation is theft! Remember the Bible declares, 'thou shalt not steal' (Ex. 20:15). If a private citizen decides to set up a printing press and make some money, he is called a criminal (counterfeiting); if the government does the same thing it is called 'monetizing the debt' or 'stimulating the economy'. What is the difference?"*[16]

Inflation discourages savings by promoting a "spend now" attitude. It encourages debt, deceives people about pay increases and future wealth accumulations, is a hidden theft tax, and decreases capital available for investment.

To get rid of inflation we should abolish the central bank, repeal all tender laws, and return to a gold warehouse receipt standard. In addition, we must also end fractional reserve banking.

Basics of Banking

Banks were places for the safe keeping of money. People who used this service paid a fee for it. Gradually, banks began to act not only as warehouses to store money, but as intermediaries between savers who were willing to lend, and other who wanted to borrow. Banks could only loan out what they had in reserve. If a bank was lending your money for you, you could not get it back until the borrower repaid it. You earned interest for your investment.

Today, most banks have a fractional reserve banking system. Banks only need to keep a small percentage of "cash" in their vaults (around 10%), and can loan the rest. This is inflationary because "money" is created through the loaning process.

Much work needs to be done to bring godly economic reform to the nations. Becoming knowledgeable of the principles of Christian ecomomics

175

is the beginning place of this reform. The next step is to instruct the citizens and leaders of a nation and then to begin to act upon these principles. The result will be a gradual increasing prosperity for the entire nation.

Chapter 13

Biblical Principles of International Relations & War

Foreign policy deals with how the people of one nation relate to the people of another nation. Today the government leaders of the various nations determine the principles of international relations and through special government officials attempt to carry on much of the outworking of the relationship.

What should be the basis of relationships between men on an international level and where are these relationships learned? Are government officials the best way to represent one nation to another?

Foreign Policy is Learned in the Home

As we mentioned in Chapter 8, the home is the first sphere of society, and hence is the first place where principles of inter-personal relations are implanted within a people. The inter-personal relations learned in the home will effect how a person relates in business, the church, organizations, and internationally.

Home is where foreign policy is learned. Home is the first war zone, in the sense that children may get into fights with one another. They learn to resolve conflicts, they learn how to work together, and they learn how to make peace. They learn how to listen to the peacemakers (Dad and Mom), as well.

The local church and church international also provides an important example for the nations of how conflicts can be resolved. Within the local church people learn how to work together with others and learn how to

177

resolve conflicts in a proper manner. The church international should show the nations that it is possible for international institutions to work together and peacefully resolve internal disputes and disagreements.

The attitudes and ideas learned in the homes (and churches and schools) of a nation concerning interpersonal relations will determine the international relations of the nation. God's law/word provides the basis for appropriate relations, not only between God and man, but also between man and man, and hence between nation and nation.

The Commandments and Foreign Policy

Jesus summarized the ten commandments in saying we should love the Lord with all our heart, soul, mind , and strength and love our neighbor as ourself. The first four commandments deal with our relationship with God, the last six with our relationship with our fellow man. To love our neighbor as ourself reveals how we are to treat neighbor nations. Examining the second table of the decalogue will give more insight into principles and attitudes we are to maintain in foreign policy. We will only briefly mention some ideas that flow from the commandments as relate to international relations.

5th Commandment - "Honor thy father and mother"

This affirms the authority of the family, and therefore, we should respect other families, which are the building blocks for races, groups, and nations, and hence, we should respect other races and nations. Any foreign policy action should never undermine the family unit as the basic building block of society.

6th Commandment - "Thou shalt not kill"

This reveals that in our dealings with other nations we must respect the life of other people. God creates all life and, therefore, life can only be taken on God's terms. Principles of war, where life may be taken, will be discussed later.

7th Commandment - "Thou shalt not commit adultery"

This command affirms the sanctity of covenants, therefore, we should respect contracts and treaties in which we engage with other nations.

8th Commandment - "Thou shalt not steal"

This command affirms the right to private property. We should respect the property rights of the citizens of other nations.

9th Commandment - "Thou shalt not bear false witness against thy neighbor."

This affirms the sanctity of truth or reputation, therefore, we should respect the reputation of other nations and not seek to take advantage of them or wrongly accuse them.

10th Commandment - "Thou shalt not covet ... any thing that is thy neighbour's."

This command affirms the sanctity of conscience. The word covet not only embrases the emotion or conscience of man, but also his action. One who covets will attempt to gain possession of, or power over, the goods and property of his neighbor or fellow man through dishonest means. In our foreign policy actions, we should respect the productivity of other nations and not seek to dishonestly gain control or possession of the property, resources, or productivity of the citizens.

The Law of Nations

Nations cannot do whatever they want, even if their law permits it. Everyone is subject to the higher law of God which is known as Creation Law or The Law of Nature. Therefore, a Christian nation must not allow other nations to violate their God-given rights. Biblical concepts of the use of force and of international Law were articulated with sound Biblical reasoning in the French Protestant document entitled *A Defense of Liberty Against Tyrants* written in 1579. But the fullest reasoning concerning a God-given Law of Nations was offered by Hugo Grotius in his book entitled *The Rights of War and Peace* written in 1625. Grotius, a Dutch lawyer, theologian, statesman and poet, has been called "the father of the modern code of nations". German thinkers Samuel Puffendorf (*The Law of Nature and Nations,* 1683) and Emerich De Vattel (*The Law of Nations*, 1758) also contributed similar Biblical reasoning.

The United States Constitution was the first national document to speak of the Law of Nations in Article 1, Section 8 where it gives Congress the right "to declare war" and "to define and punish Piracies and Felonies committed on the high Seas, and Offences against the Law of Nations."

John Eidsmoe writes:

> *"The United States established war tribunals to bring foreign officials to trial for atrocities committed in violation of the Law of Nations or international law, based on this clause of the Constitution. The fact that such officials could be held to a higher standard of conduct and that simple 'obedience to orders' was not considered an absolute defense to charges of violating international law, indicates further recognition that the laws of man are subject to the law of God."*[1]

There is nothing inherently wrong with the concept of nations working together to punish aggressors and international criminals such as is being attempted today in the United Nations (and even uniting their economic systems such as is being attempted today in the European Community). A "New World Order" that is based on a truly Biblical idea of Law, man and government, and economics is a fine goal and should not be rejected automatically. However, the pagan tendency to centralize everything leads to tyranny and should be avoided in terms of actual governmental powers being united and national sovereignty being surrendered. The critical need is for no compromise on Biblical ideas of government.

What the Bible Says about War

In our brief look at this topic we will be offering Biblical ideas, not necessarily every "Christian" idea or opinion. While Biblical interpretation of the subject of war has varied over the years the Scriptural perspectives presented here are also supported by the major, orthodox, historic Christian traditions.

God's Original Intention For Human Affairs

God originally created a world without sin and violence which meant a world needing no civil government, at least as we know it today (Gen 1:26,31). A world without sin and violence meant a world without crime and punishment, police forces, military forces or war.

How Sin Changed God's Original Intention

The first man, Adam, rebelled against God and no man ever since has ever exhibited a sinless nature (Rom 5:12,14). The first violent act was when Cain killed Abel (Gen 4:8). The sin nature of man without any external restraints led to a world of runaway violence and murder (Gen 6:11-13).

While this section will focus mostly on the way in which we must deal with such a sinful world, the Bible urges us to place our central focus on the hope of a future without war (Isa. 2:4; Isa. 60:18; Rev 21:4).

God started the world over and established civil government delegating to it the power of force ("sword")(Gen. 6:17,18; Gen. 9:1,5,6). The purpose was two-fold: 1. To protect innocent, defenseless people by the threat of punishment of those who assault others (Rom 13:3,4). 2. To punish those who fail to restrain themselves and commit an evil, unjust act against another person (1 Pet. 2:13,14).

The foundational reasoning for government, capital punishment, and defensive war, therefore, comes from the value that God places on innocent human life. Those who violate the sanctity of human life through murder, forfeit their own protection (Gen. 9:6).

There are two types of killing:

1. Killing of innocent people (i.e. murder). This is unjust, unlawful, and unsanctioned by God (Ex 20:13).

2. Killing of people guilty of crimes against others (i.e. capital punishment). This is just, lawful and sanctioned by God (Ex 21:12). This must be carried out, however, only in two ways in order to be just. The first is by government authorities after due process of law. This is why Jesus did not condone capital punishment against the woman accused of adultery (Deut 17:4-7; John 8:4,5,7). She had not been provided a fair hearing according to Biblical standards. The second way in which killing is just is by individuals being assaulted who defend their lives with force. This, however, must still be examined by government authorities to determine that it was indeed warranted (Ex 22:2). This law also presupposes the right to bear arms.

Types of War

There are two types of war. One is aggression arising out of greed, lust, pride, etc. This is unjust, unlawful, and unsanctioned by God (James 4:1,2). The second is that which arises out of a need to defend against the aggressor.

This is just, lawful and sanctioned by God (Num. 31:1-3; Neh. 4:14; Rom. 13:4).

Biblical Principles of Warfare

Not only must war be based on Biblical and just grounds, but it must also be conducted within Biblical guidelines or else it is immoral. The Bible provides explicit principles of warfare in Deuteronomy chapter 20 and other places. Some of those basic elements are:

1. Target the leadership/crush the head

The Bible holds the leaders of society primarily responsible for social decisions. Thus, the most important matter in victory over an invading army is the destruction of its leadership. Assassination of the heads of the enemy state is a Biblical principle of war (Judges; In 1 Sam 15:8,9 King Saul is stripped of his position because of his failure to kill King Agag). It is more just than killing the members of the enemy army because the head is responsible; plus it is simpler and less costly.

2. Continually offer peace through negotiation (Deut 20:10ff; Luke 14:31,32)

3. The land and innocent civilians are not to be destroyed

Warfare is not to be waged against everything and everyone in the enemy nation (Deut 20:19,20). The "trees" here may also refer to men (Psa 1 and Judges 9).

4. Universal participation of all men under age 20 (Judges 21; 8:4-17; 5:23).

Whole groups may not excuse themselves, however, clergy (Num 1:48,49), a man engaged to be married or is building a house (Deut 20:5-8; 24:5), and those who admit to being fearful (Deut 20:8; Judges 7:3) may exempt themselves.

5. Localism, not a national army

Those near the battle are expected to send more men and support the war more heavily than those farther away. Some token of support, however, should come from everywhere.

6. Chaplains are to be provided to comfort the dying and fearful and also to inspire and encourage before battle with messages.

7. Small professional force allowed but mostly a militia army led by local leaders.

Israel did not have a large permanent national professional army. A small professional force to use as bodyguards and as emergency troops until the militia arrives is okay (1 Sam. 8:11; 1 Chron. 21 and 27; 1 Sam. 23:13).

8. The members of a militia provide their own weapons that a common soldier would use (1 Sam 25:13; Num 31:3; 32:20). It is unbiblical and tends toward tyranny if only a king and his professional army have weapons (Judges 5:8; 1 Sam 13:19-22).

9. A militia is to be led by local officers elected by the people who have the right to refuse service if it is an unbiblical war (1 Kings 12; Deut 20:9; Num 31:4,14).

10. No aggression allowed (i.e. no horses and chariots allowed for the king's use (Deut 17:16; 1 Sam 8:11).

The Nature of Jesus Christ when it comes to the use of force.

We shall not attempt to present all the examples that Christ gave of forgiveness, peace, and love, but assume that most people already know of this aspect of Christ's nature. To have an accurate perception of Jesus, be sure to keep these in mind as you examine the following examples.

1. Jesus said that He was a part of the triune Godhead, one with the Father, and therefore equally a party to all examples of punishment and war that God sanctioned in the Old Testament (Heb. 1:3 & 13:8; John 8:58).

2. Jesus made a whip Himself one time and used force to turn over tables and chairs in order to drive merchants out of the Temple. Then He forcibly blocked access (John 2:15; Mark 11:16).

3. Jesus asserted one time that He did not come to bring peace but a "sword" (Matt 10:34).

4. Jesus carried out the instant judgement pronounced by Peter in His name against Ananias and Sapphira under the New Covenant (Acts 5:9,10).

5. Jesus Himself and the New Testament Scriptures say that Jesus will be "taking vengeance on those who do not know God" and will slay the ungodly at the end of time (2 Thess. 1:7-9; Rev. 19:11,15,21).

What Jesus specifically taught about weapons and war

1. He directly commanded His followers to arm themselves with weapons (Luke 22:36,38).

By referring to His earlier teaching where He explained how to protect their liberties first by protest and then by fleeing (Luke 22:35; Luke 10:10,11; Matt 10:23), Jesus was thereby conveying the principle that force was only to be used as the third step or last resort after all previous means were exhausted (Deut 20:10). The Old Testament laws of war required attempts at negotiation before beginning battle (Deut 20:10).

2. He distinguished between weapons used in aggression and weapons used in self-defense (Matt. 26:51,52).

Jesus rebuked Peter only for taking an offensive action with the sword. He did not say that all uses of the sword were unjust. Jesus said rather that the unjust use of the sword in aggression is judged by God not directly from heaven but through others who use the sword justly in self-defense.

3. He distinguished between mere insult and life threatening force (Matt 5:39).

If you are slapped with an open hand you should swallow your pride, turn the other cheek and "love" your enemy. But Christ does not make such a requirement if the hand is closed into a fist or other more lethal force is used. Still, the motive for resistance should not be "evil for evil" but only a just self-preservation.

4. He distinguished between the usefulness of weapons for earthly kingdoms from His heavenly kingdom (John 18:36).

Jesus never condemns the use of weapons on an earthly level but rather endorses their legitimacy for nations to protect their liberty. But He clearly affirms that the Kingdom of God is advanced differently - only by the "sword of the Spirit" which is the preaching of the Word of God (Eph 6:17). The apostle Paul saw nothing wrong in the aid of the military when they rescued him from those who opposed his ministry and wanted to kill him, but Paul never asked soldiers to help him force people to believe the Gospel (Acts 21:31,32,35).

5. He never taught any of the soldiers that sought His input to leave their military profession, but instead even praised them (Luke 7:8,9).

In their ministries Jesus, John the Baptist, and the Apostles all responded to those who asked what they must do to be right with God. Sometimes they urged restitution by tax-gatherers, or commanded others to sin no more, but never was a military man told to not use arms in any way. In fact, the Bible calls Cornelius, a military man by profession, a "just man" and one who feared God (Luke 3:14; Acts 10:22). The heroes of the faith recorded in Hebrews 11:34 include those who "became valiant in battle and turned to flight the armies of the aliens". David was a military man and yet was said to be a man "after God's own heart".

6. Jesus commanded to "render to Caesar the things that are Caesar's" (Matt 22:21).

Caesar required two things of the citizen: pay taxes and serve in the military. Jesus clearly affirmed the payment of taxes and also never denied that military service was legitimate.

7. Jesus taught that peace comes through strength of arms (Luke 11:21,22; Luke 14:31).

An attack usually comes if the aggressor perceives that he is "stronger" militarily, and therefore it is best to have a fully armed house (or nation).

The example of Israel, as well as nations throughout history, reveal that a nation can only have liberty and peace through strength. America's Founders agreed. George Washington, America's first president, said: *"There is a rank due to the United States among nations, which will be withheld, if not absolutely lost, by the reputation of weakness. If we desire to avoid insult, we must be able to repel it; if we desire peace... it must be known that we are at all times ready for war."* He also stated, *"To be prepared for war is one of the most effectual means of preserving peace."*[2]

Thomas Jefferson wrote: *"Whatever enables us to go to war, secures our peace."*[3]

A Christian Foreign Policy

Although the Bible provides for a just use of force as a deterrent in a sinful world, it goes on and also provides a glorious promise of a world without war. There are prophecies of world peace. Some feel these will not be fully achieved until the end of time and the return of Christ. Others feel that these are achievable in human history.

The only way to achieve any degree of peace on earth is through first changing the human heart, which will solve the sin and greed problem. This happens through regeneration available through faith in Christ (Tit. 3:1-6; 1 Cor. 6:9-11). Secondly, men's minds must be renewed through education in Biblical principles of war and peace. The influence of Christian ideas of man and government can help diminish the pagan model of centralized political power and aggression among the nations (Matt. 28:19,20; Rom. 12:2; Micah 4:2,3).

185

Just, defensive war is simply a stop-gap necessity in a sinful world until the above is achieved. The primary hope and goal of world peace should be where our energy and work is directed.

A Christian nation should relate to foreign nations in much the same way a Christian should relate to an unbeliever. We are to be peacemakers, mercy-givers, teachers, and defenders of the helpless and the oppressed. We should not try to impose our will upon other nations, but we should sow the truth within the heart of the people in a nation, knowing that this internal change will affect the public affairs of a nation.

In George Washington's *Farewell Address* in 1796, he set forth some basic principles of a proper foreign policy. These include:

1. Cultivate peace with all nations and maintain impartiality

"Observe good faith and justice towards all nations; cultivate peace and harmony with all. Religion and morality enjoin this conduct....It will be worthy of a free, enlightened, and...great nation to give to mankind the...novel example of a people always guided by an exalted justice and benevolence....

"Harmony, liberal intercourse with all nations, are recommended by policy, humanity, and interest."

"In the execution of such a plan nothing is more essential than that permanent, inveterate antipathies against particular nations, and passionate attachments for others, should be excluded; and that, in place of them, just and amicable feelings towards all should be cultivated. The nation which indulges towards another an habitual hatred, or an habitual fondness, is in some degree a slave. It is a slave to its animosity or to its affection, either of which is sufficient to lead it astray from its duty and its interest. Antipathy in one nation against another disposes each more readily to offer insult and injury, to lay hold of slight causes of umbrage, and to be haughty and intractable, when accidental or trifling occasions of dispute occur. Hence, frequent collisions, obstinate, envenomed and bloody contests. The nation, prompted by ill will and resentment, sometimes impels to war the government, contrary to the best calculations of policy. The government sometimes participates in the national propensity, and adopts through passion what reason would reject; at other times, it makes the animosity of the nation subservient to projects of hostility instigated by pride, ambition, and other sinister and pernicious motives. The peace often, sometimes perhaps the liberty, of nations has been the victim.

"So, likewise, a passionate attachment of one nation for another produces a variety of evils. Sympathy for the favorite nation, facilitating the illusion of an imaginary common interest, in cases where no real common interest exists, and infusing into one the enmities of the other, betrays the former into a participation in the quarrels and wars of the latter without adequate inducement or justification. It leads, also, to concessions to the favorite nation of privileges denied to others, which is apt doubly to injure the nation making the concessions; by unnecessarily parting with what ought to have been retained; and by exciting jealousy, ill will, and a disposition to retaliate in the parties from whom equal privileges are withheld."

2. With trading, keep political connections to a minimum.

"The great rule of conduct for us, in regard to foreign nations, is, in extending our commercial relations, to have with them as little political connections as possible.... But, even our commercial policy should hold an equal and impartial hand; neither seeking nor granting exclusive favors or preferences; consulting the natural course of things...constantly keeping in view, that it is folly in one nation to look for disinterested favors from another; that it must pay with a portion of its independence for whatever it may accept under that character..."

It should be left entirely to the private sector to decide who to trade with, not the government. However, if our national security is threatened, trade can and should be limited.

3. No long-term entangling alliances.

"It is our true policy to steer clear of permanent alliances with any portion of the foreign world.... taking care always to keep ourselves by suitable establishments, on a respectable defensive posture, we may safely trust to temporary alliances for extraordinary emergencies."

Gary North defines these "permanent alliances" that Washington warned against as *"the creation of international treaties that would bind together the United States and other nations to perform certain military actions under specified future circumstances."* [4]

The main points were summarized by **Jefferson** in his First Inaugural Address:

"Peace, Commerce, and Honest Friendship with all nations, entangling alliances with none."

A nation that shows impartiality toward all nations and does not engage in long-term entangling alliances would be in a position to be an example to other nations and in this way positively affect them. If a Christian nation treats all nations equally, and does not attempt to act as the policemen of the world, then the nations will more readily seek their advice and judgement, allowing that nation to sow Christian truth within them.

Intervention Should Be Based on Just Principles

The cause of those nations which seek intervention by another nation should be based on just principles (on the Christian idea of man and government). We must realize that no nation perfectly adheres to these principles, but that should be the desire.

Therefore, the basis for one nation becoming involved in the affairs of another nation includes: 1) Legitimate officials ask for help. 2) A nation's own security or self-preservation is threatened by action in another. 3) Their cause is based on just principles. If it is determined that it is legitimate to give assistance, then the type of aid must be decided, whether money, goods, weapons, troops, etc. Complete isolationism in international affairs is no more Biblical than it would be for an individual who sees a weak person being assaulted by a larger, brutal person to just look the other way and pretend it wasn't happening. A just war does not have to be limited to being a defensive one; it can be conducted on the basis of avenging bloodshed (Judges 19-21).

In providing aid to needy nations, we should not attempt to merely throw money at their acute problems, especially if there is little understanding of Christian self-government in these lands. Aid to nations must be encouraged and overseen by our government, but it should not come from public money, since God did not create government to provide welfare, only promote it. International aid should be provided by private businesses investing in other countries, and by charitable Christian missions work. Christian businessmen should be transplanters of prosperity all over the world, demonstrating through their actions what the free market can do. This would do more for poverty stricken nations than giving them a free lunch that they will mismanage in the same way that caused their poverty in the first place. This would also prevent a governmental "imperialistic" attitude of domination among nations and help governments to treat each other with greater respect. If a fraction of the government resources now spent on military hardware was spent on colonizing the ideas of the Bible, a proper foundation would be laid for the development of liberty and self-government in other lands.

Missionaries and Christian businessmen should be the ambassadors of Christian nations.

Today, it is erroneously believed that only professional diplomats who have legal and governmental and political training are qualified to serve as ambassadors to foreign countries.

Gary North writes:

"In the field of international relations, no one before this era [the 20th century] had perceived a need for the United States government to send official representatives to every nation or to seek alliances, agreements, and arrangements with every nation. People assumed that private interests would be the basis of the vast bulk of international relations."[5]

This is the heart of the problem in foreign policy, today. North says that, *"Voters in the West have passively turned over the conduct of foreign policy to professional diplomats."*[6] Now, you may ask: If professional diplomats aren't supposed to be conducting foreign policy, then who is? Lee grady writes:

"Practically, foreign policy in this Christian world order will be conducted by missionaries and members of the Christian business and trade community who know how to represent the cause of Christ abroad. Their business as ambassadors of Christ is not to work out terms of compromise; it is to persuade men and governments to surrender to the government of Christ.

"The prophet Isaiah spoke of a progressive, worldwide surrender to the gospel when he wrote: 'The law will go forth from Zion... and He [God] will judge between the nations, and will render decisions for many peoples; and they will hammer their swords into plowshares, and their spears into pruning hooks. Nation will not lift up sword against nation, and never again will they learn war'(Isaiah 2:4).

"It is important to note that the act of transforming swords into plowshares takes place after the peoples of the earth voluntarily confess, 'Come and let us go unto the mountain of the Lord, that He may teach us His ways' (v. 3). God is waiting for knees to bow in submission before He resolves international conflict. That is His condition for peace.

"North summarizes this idea: 'There can never be peace in history outside of Christ. There can be temporary cease-fire agreements, but never a lasting peace. What Christians must understand is that peace is attained through the preaching of the gospel and the discipling of the nations. There is no other way. God will not permit peace on any other terms....'"

"To the humanist, peace is really pacifism. My dictionary accurately defines pacifism as 'opposition to war or to the use of military force for any purpose; an attitude of mind opposing all war and advocating settlement of international disputes entirely by arbitration'... The current 'Peace studies' programs in U.S. colleges should be called pacifism majors. No professor in any of these universities is offering any way to achieve peace according to the true definition." [7]

This kind of pacifism is not even rooted in the conscientious pacifism that is sincerely held by some Christians. Although this chapter has taught that pacifism is not in line with a thorough Biblical study of war and government, nonetheless, anyone who believes that it is against their conscience to participate in war should not be punished, but allowed to refuse military service (Deut 20:1-8; Judges 7:3). This was done in the Hebrew Republic and, therefore, is the Biblical response toward those who feel this way. Clearly, the emphasis that Christian pacifists place on world peace and nonviolence is a goal we should work and pray for according to the Bible. However, in a fallen, sinful world this is unachieveable. Until the return of Christ and the removal of evil from the world, men will have need of the use of the sword to restrain violent aggressive acts. The Bible affirms such use is legitimate.

Chapter 14

A Practical Agenda for Discipling a Nation

This chapter will offer a summary of the key points mentioned in this book that deal with a Biblical philosophy and strategic action that is necessary for effectively liberating the nations. This chapter will also present Biblical methods for positive social change that have not been mentioned before.

As we discussed in Chapter 6, Jesus Christ emphasized the necessity for resisting evil and addressing injustice using the Biblical means of (1) Protest, (2) Flight/emigration, (3) Force in self Defence. But Jesus went even further and called on His followers to overcome evil with good. In other words, you cannot beat something with nothing. Anyone can be a critic, but our culture needs Christian statesmen and social reformers like the prophets of the Bible who spoke up and took action to alleviate the needs of suffering men. Jesus taught that there is a time when one should get involved in the legal and political system in order to defend one's rights and to address injustice. Luke 18:2-5 primarily teaches us about persistence in prayer, yet is based on a civil setting for achieving justice which Christ clearly affirms. It is not unbiblical to pursue social influence by legal means through the courts or by "occupying" (i.e. getting involved in) the governmental systems that already exist (Luke 19:11-17).

Biblical methods for positive social change are:

1. Education (Matt 28:19)

Jesus gave Christians the primary way to "disciple the nations" when He commanded His disciples in Matthew 28:19 to go and "teach".

What was it that the church was to teach? "All that I commanded you". Let us review exactly what Jesus taught in relation to nations' civil affairs:

1. Gradual Democratic Change/Internal to the External
2. Civil Government is a Divinely Ordained Institution
3. Limited Government/Jurisdictional Boundaries
4. The Inherent Value of the Individual/Diversity
5. Government is to Serve All Men Equally
6. The Civil Laws of Moses/Fundamental Rights
7. Use Biblical Political Means to Achieve Social Justice

The means for educating the community in a biblical worldview:

Homes

The Bible teaches the family is always the primary provider of education. Parents should establish a regular Sabbath day time for instructing their children in the Christian history of their family, church, and nation. They should have a regular Bible-devotional time each day, plus, a reading-aloud program in great Christian literature. The family should also do as much of the education of their children as possible at home, and whatever they cannot provide, they should seek to work in voluntary union with other home-schooling parents and church leaders to provide coordinated tutoring or to set up Christian schools.

Churches

Like the Levites in the Hebrew Republic and the Clergy in Britain and the United States, the Pastors and ministers and priests today must begin a regular program of discipleship for their members either through a weekly class for adults or through home-groups/special study groups that are set up for this purpose in the congregation. Near election times or around special community events and national holidays, special sermons should be preached. These election and commemorative sermons can be preached on Sundays at church or at special seminars for the general community. Distributing these sermons in printed form will help disseminate the truth.

In addition to this, the church should try to help supplement the schooling efforts of parents by starting private schools or by coordinating special tutoring and events for home-schooling parents. Clergy should also be accessible to community leaders in the government, business, and media spheres so as to provide consultation and advise from a Biblical perspective.

Media and the Arts

The Prophets of the Bible and Christians throughout the centuries have led the way in communications. They should once again work together in voluntary union to publish books and newspapers from a Biblical worldview. Radio, television, and movies should also be recaptured by consistent service in already existing institutions, but also by creating new television networks and movie production companies that do more than just "religious" programming. They should start new News Networks on radio and television to give commentary on everyday affairs from a Christian perspective.

Schools and Colleges

Besides the family returning to home-schooling, Christians should work to start private schools available to all people, and in so doing keep the government out of education. This means that enough quality schools must be opened to meet the needs of everyone, including those children of poor, non-Christian families that cannot or will not home-school or start their own private schools. Additionally, Christians should recapture the Universities, especially those which were started by Christians originally, through consistent service in them. Christians should also start new colleges and universities, like Samuel's School of the Prophets (2 Kg. 13:14 and 1 Sam 19:20) and Ezekiel's synagogues, which teach a Biblical worldview.

2. Campaigning to elect Godly representatives

The Apostle Paul rebuked the Corinthian Christians in Greece for allowing the civil courts and government positions to be controlled by pagans (1 Cor 6:2-5). This rebuke was appropriate because in Greece the citizens could choose some of their civil officials. In a democratic system of government, to neglect to put Christians in places of leadership is a sin just as it would be to hide our talents as Jesus spoke of in Matthew 25:14-30. This is a basic part of a citizen's duty in a Biblical democratic government (Exod 18 and Deut 1). Every Christian is called to select godly representatives, not just a few. There are only two possibilities for every Christian to consider: Assisting and serving others who seek office, or running for public office yourself.

Christians who do nothing will give an account to God for their neglect of a biblical command (Those Christians living in countries where there is still not the freedom of elections will be accountable to God for their efforts to bring it about).

How can one expect to have good government if righteous people with a Biblical worldview do not run for office or if Christians are apathetic and not involved. To leave "party politics" to only those few Christians who "are called" to do so is a deception to excuse our own neglect of duty. Certainly only a few are genuinely called by God to run for public office, but every Christian is called to help them in some way. It is this neglect of Biblical duty that allows the ungodly to gain control of government and for corruption to come in free nations, bringing national judgement and sorrow upon our children.

The Bible is full of examples of God's people helping their brethren to get in public office. Samuel campaigned for Saul to be King, and later for David to be King, by anointing them, and thus publicly promoting them (1 Sam. 16:1,2).

Nathan did likewise for Solomon (1 Kings 1:32-34). Ahijah did the same for Jeroboam (1 Kings 11:26-39; 12:12-15). Elisha encouraged Jehu to unseat King Ahab and Queen Jezebel (2 Kings 9:1,6,7,10,21,30,33).

The prophets of the Bible cannot be understood apart from their political and social activity to bring reform in their nation. The overwhelming majority of their attention and messages were toward government leaders and social problems. Prophets were simply statesmen or social reformers; political activists whether for good (God's prophets) or for bad (false prophets). A false prophet is simply one who works for social reform based on a pagan philosphy of life. A true prophet is one who bases his ideas and political activities on a Biblical worldview.

There have been many other prophets throughout the Christian era. They did not cease with the Old Testament. They have already been mentioned in the earlier chapters of this book. Men who campaigned for and assisted righteous leaders to win public office were: Stephen Langton who helped the English Barons, and John Wycliffe and Jan Hus in Europe; and John Witherspoon, Charles Finney, and John Wesley in the United States.

Many of God's people in the Bible and throughout history have actually sought Public Office. The Bible speaks of two ministries ordained by God: the gospel minister and the civil minister (Rom 13:4). Since they are both ministries of God, Erastus, a full-time apostolic assistant to Paul, easily switches to become the Commissioner of Public Works in the city of Corinth to set an example that Paul was serious about Christians seeking public office (Acts 19:22; Rom 16:23).

Clergy in the Old Testament also sought public office, such as in the case of Samuel, Ezra, and Zephaniah and a host of other Levites who served as civil officials (Deut 17:8-13; 2 Chr 19:8,11). But God's people who were not necessarily clergy by profession also served in government: Noah, Abraham, Isaac, and Jacob were Patriarchal princes. Joseph became the Prime Minister of Egypt. Moses, Joshua, Deborah, David, Zerubbabel, Nehemiah, Esther (Queen in Persia), Mordecai and Daniel (in Persian and Babylonian governents) are other examples.

The American preacher of the 19th century, Charles Finney, wrote in his *Revivals of Religion* that one of the things that must be done to assure the continuamce of revival was this:

> "The Church must take right ground in regard to politics.... The time has come that Christians must vote for honest men, and take consistent ground in politics, or the Lord will curse them.... God cannot sustain this free and blessed country, which we love and pray for, unless the Church will take right ground. Politics are a part of a religion in such a country as this, and Christians must do their duty to the country as a part of their duty to God.... He [God] will bless or curse this nation, according to the course they [Christians] take [in politics]."[1]

3. Influencing Leaders

Christians have a duty to educate their civil rulers in Biblical truths. Whether the ruler in power is a Christian or not makes no difference on whether a Christian should be trying to sway his decisions toward a Biblical worldview. This can be done in two ways: Either by gaining direct access as an advisor within the government, or by serving the needs of special groups that select you as their spokesman to government.

Most of us will not be able to be an advisor to a ruler, so let us first look at the call to special advocacy of people groups in need of help (Luke 19:13; Prov 31:8,9; 1 Sam 8:9). Elisha was an excellent example of this. He served people throughout the nation of Israel with legitimate needs and thus became one with influence on the government.

There were many individuals in the Bible who became direct close advisors to government rulers (1 Kings 1:5,11-14) such as: Samuel, Nathan, Gad, Jeduthun, Ahijah, Elisha, Azariah, Jahaziel, Zephaniah, Huldah, Daniel, Haggai, Zechariah, Esther, Ezra, and Malachi. Even Paul in the New Testament counseled government rulers that he was around, like Sergius Paulus the Roman proconsul in Acts 13:6-7. Probably the Bible's greatest example of an advisory role to rulers was Isaiah. In Chapters 29-35 and 36-39 Isaiah is seen providing advice to King Hezekiah that dramatically influenced the nation concerning war plans, alliances, and other affairs.

Another way in which advice is given is in an opposing confrontive rebuke rather than as an advisor to a ruler. The instances of this in the Bible is voluminous. The prophets Jeremiah and John the Baptist are two of the many examples.

4. Providing Alternative Services

A third positive and constructive method of social change is the building of models of social services by the private sector - Church, Business, Family - which operate on a Biblical approach to solving problems. These will better meet the needs of the people. When the social needs start being met more effectively, then people will come to you, which will gradually influence the way others are meeting those needs, since they will have to change in order to compete. Social services to the poor and needy are best modeled by Christians working in voluntary union (Eph 6; Philemon; Acts 15:2,4,6; 5:14; James 2; and 3:9).

Some Unbiblical Methods of Political Action:

1. Tax evasion (except perhaps in countries where there are no free elections allowing citizens to change the law).
2. Referendums (bypassing the legislature is dangerous democracy, but may be necessary if the people have little voice in the political parties).

3. Amendments to the Constitution that are misplaced (i.e. trying to bring social change by external methods only, instead of using internal change through revival and moral education).

4. Using government funding. (It is unbiblical for government to dispense special welfare, even for good causes.)

5. Censorship (government coerced restriction of art and books).

6. Deception

7. Slander or a "party spirit." (Unwholesome or untrue words spoken publicly about another person or group is not Biblical.)

8. Force without government authorization.

9. Government redistribution of wealth.

10. Starting new political parties is not unbiblical but may be unnecessary as long as existing parties have a decent reputation and are open to participation by anyone (but if existing parties are closed, Christians should start new ones).

Practical Steps For Action According to Spheres

Individuals:

1. Attend church regularly and support it with your resources and efforts at proclamation of the gospel to unbelieving friends.

2. Seek a good job and labor conscientiously to express the Kingdom of God in that setting.

3. Contribute part of your income to needy individuals and agencies.

4. Obtain weapons to defend yourself if necessary.

5. Faithfully express dissent and protest injustice .

6. Pray for revival and righteous government.

7. Attend (or start) a neighborhood political/service group.

8. Avoid consumer debt and seek investors for business ventures instead of borrowing.

9. Have a savings program.

Families

1. Be fruitful and multiply; have children.

2. Take responsibility for educating your children through home-schooling and supplementary tutoring, or through private schools.

3. Have regular Bible-devotions and read aloud to your children from classic Christian literature.

4. Save and invest in means of health care for yourself and your family and open your home to grandparents and relatives.

5. Consider the Biblical example of designating an extra portion of your estate to go one child who will care for you in retirement.

6. Establish a "loving trust" to provide an inheritance for your children before you die.

7. Have a regular sabbath tradition for remembering God's hand in the history of your family, church and nation.

8. Start new universities and media outlets and encourage arts with a Godly foundation.

Governments:

1. Shut down public schools and Government Departments of Education. (This will occur gradually as parents, churches, and the private sector assumes their responsibility.)

2. Cease funding all special interests, health & welfare. (Aspects of this may have to be done gradually, as others assume the responsibility.)

3. Establish a civilian army and police force with only a small number of professional soldiers (have elected officers).

4. Establish laws by community concensus against pornography, abortion, homosexuality, no-fault divorce, etc.

6. Allow non-denominational religion in public settings.

7. Prohibit the government from controlling wages and prices, spending more than it takes in, and taxing unbiblically.

8. Prohibit the government from long-term treaties and imperialistic foreign affairs. Deputize missionaries and businessmen to be ambassadors.

Churches:

1. Have a regular teaching/discipling program on the responsibilities of Individuals, Families, Citizens, and Rulers.

2. Coordinate charitable giving and activities and evangelism and education.

3. Start City Action Councils to unite the churches in one city-wide long-term plan.

4. Fulfill regular ecclesiastical functions (e.g. administer the Lord's supper and baptism).

5. Educate the general public in Biblical ideas through literature distribution and seminars, etc.

6. Be a model of equality, morality, etc.

7. Be available to serve government, business and media leaders.

All individuals and institutions should work to establish or restore the seven Biblical structures of government (i.e. have a Christian form of government):

1. Decentralization of Power and government

2. Three branches or functions of government

3. Written constitutions

4. Independent Judiciary and trial by jury

5. Civilian Police and militia (right to own weapons)

6. Election of Representatives

7. Separation of Government from Religion, Market, Press & Schools

More importantly, we should work to infuse the seven fundamental principles into the hearts of the all the people (i.e. have a Christian power as the support of society):

1. Christian Self-Government

2. Christian Union

3. Individuality

4. Property/Conscience

5. Christian Education

6. Christian Character

7. Faith in God and His Word

Footnotes

Chapter 1

1. Francis A. Schaeffer, *How Should We Then Live?* (New Jersey, 1976), p. 23.
2. Rosalie J. Slater, *Teaching and Learning America's Christian History* (San Francisco, 1980), p. 119.
3. Russ Walton, *One Nation Under God* (Nashville, 1987), p. 19.
4. *The Christian History of the Constitution of the United States of America*, compiled by Verna M. Hall (San Francisco, 1980), pp. 16-17. [designated CHOC in future references]
5. John Locke, *Of Civil Government*, quoted in CHOC, p. 58.
6. Slater, p. 251.
7. Noah Webster, *History of the United States* (New Haven, 1833), pp. 273-274.

Chapter 2

1. Peter Marshall and David Manuel, *The Light and the Glory* (New Jersey, 1977), p. 370.
2. David Barret, *Cosmos, Chaos, and Gospel, a Chronology of World Evangelization from Creation to New Creation* (Birmingham, Al., 1987).
3. Charles Rollin, *The Ancient History of the Egyptians, Carthaginians, Assyrians, Babylonians, Medes and Persians, Grecians, and Macedonians; including a History of the Arts and Sciences of the Ancients.* 2 volumes (New York, 1836.
4. Rev. S.W. Foljambe, "The Hand of God in American History," Annual Election Sermon, Boston, Mass., January 5, 1876, quoted in *The Christian History of the American Revolution, Consider and Ponder,* Verna M. Hall, compiler (San Francisco, 1976), p. 47. [designated Consider and Ponder in future footnotes]

5. Ibid., p. 46.
6. See CHOC for concept of Chain of Christianity.

Chapter 3

1. Richard Frothingham, *The Rise of the Republic of the United States*, quoted in CHOC, p. 1.
2. Ibid., p. 2.
3. Figures from David Barret.
4. *Eerdmans' Handbook to the Bible,* Edited by David Alexander and Pat Alexander (Grand Rapids, 1973), p. 588.
5. For more on the Celtic Church see, Leslie Hardinge, *The Celtic Church in Britain*, London: Church Historical Society, 1973.
6. David Chilton, "Alfred the Great," in Equity, Christian Public Policy Council, Jan. 1989, p. 3.
7. W. Cleon Skousen, *The Making of America* (Washington, D.C., 1985), p. 32.
8. G.V. Lechler, *John Wycliffe and His English Precursors,* quoted in Slater, p. 167.
9. Ibid., p. 168.

Chapter 4

1. Charles Carleton Coffin, *The Story of Liberty* (New York, 1878), p. 79.
2. Christopher Columbus, *Book of Prophecies,* translated into English by Kay Brigham (Barcelona, 1991).
3. Daniel Dorchester, *Christianity in the United States* (New York, 1895), p. 24.
4. B.F. Morris, *Christian Life and Character of the Civil Institutions of the United States* (Philadelphia, 1864), pp. 41-42.
5. Henry C. Sheldon, *History of the Christian Church*, quoted in Slater, p. 169.
6. J.H. Merle D'Aubigne, *History of the Reformation in Europe*, quoted in Slater, p. 171.
7. Ibid., pp. 170-171.
8. Ibid., p. 171.
9. This and following quotes on Tyndale from D'Aubigne, quoted in Slater, pp. 334-336.
10. John Overton Choules, *Preface* to the 1844 reprint of Neal's *History of*

the *Puritans*, quoted in CHOC, p. 183.

11. *A Selection of the Principal Voyages, Traffiques and Discoveries of the English Nation by Richard Hakluyt, 1552-1616*, compiled by Laurence Irving (New York, 1926), pp. 285, 291.

12. Hakluyt, p. 291.

13. This and the following quotes are from Coffin, pp. 330, 335. See also John Motley's *Rise of the Dutch Republic*.

Chapter 5

1. Rousas John Rushdoony, *The Institutes of Biblical Law*, The Presbyterian and Reformed Publishing Co., 1973, p. 1.

2. William Bradford, *Of Plimoth Plantation* (Boston, 1928), pp. 12-13.

3. Bradford, p. 32.

4. Bradford, p. 110.

5. Robert Winthrop, "A Model of Christian Charity," Old South Leaflets, Old South Meeting House, Boston.

6. John Fiske, *The Beginnings of New England* (Boston, 1898), p. 137.

7. Fiske, pp. 137, 140

8. Morris, p. 69.

9. Morris, pp. 98-101.

10. Mark A. Beliles and Stephen K. McDowell, *America's Providential History* (Charlottesville, 1989), p. 88-89.

11. Ibid. p. 90.

12. Morris, p. 56.

13. Marshall and Manuel, p. 309.

14. John Wingate Thorton, *The Pulpit of the American Revolution* (Boston, 1860).

15. Beliles and McDowell, p. 178.

Chapter 6

1. Augustus Neander, *General History of the Christian Religion and Church*, quoted in Slater, p. 213.

2. Ibid., p. 214.

3. Quoted in Norman Cousins, *In God We Trust* (New York, 1958), p. 368.

Chapter 7

1. William V. Wells, *The Life and Public Services of Samuel Adams, Vol. 3* (Boston, 1865), p. 301.
2. Noah Webster, *An American Dictionary of the English Language,* original 1828 version republished in facsimile edition by Foundation for American Christian Education (San Francisco, 1980).
3. Slater, p. 88.
4. *Consider and Ponder*, pp. 605-606.
5. Slater, pp. 278-279.
6. Morris, p. 72.
7. Noah Webster, "Education of Youth in America," American Magazine (March 1788):212. Quoted in *Defining Noah Webster, Mind and Morals in the Early Republic,* by K. Alan Snyder, New York: University Press of America, 1990, p. 114.

Chapter 8

1. Slater, p. 3.
2. Rev. S. Phillips, *The Christian Home as it is in the Sphere of Nature and the Church,* quoted in Slater, p. 7.
3. Phillips, quoted in Slater, p. 11.
4. *The Works of Daniel Webster,* Vol. 2, Boston: Little, Brown, & Co., 1854, pp. 107-108.
5. Lydia H. Sigourney, *Letters to Young Ladies* (1852), quoted in CHOC, pp. 407-410.
6. Morris.
7. CHOC, p. 273.
8. Samuel Blumenfeld, *Is Public Education Necessary?* (Boise, 1985), pp. 19-20.
9. Samuel Blumenfeld, *N.E.A. - Trojan Horse in American Education* (Boise, 1985).

Chapter 9

1. Alexis de Tocqueville, *Democracy in America,* edited by J.P. Mayer (Garden City, NY, 1969).
2. Skousen, p. 679.

3. Thorton, quoted in *Consider and Ponder,* pp. 191-192.
4. Norman V. Pope, "Educator, Minister, Patriot," in *Nation Under God,* ed. Frances Brentano (Great Neck, New York, 1957), pp. 41-42.
5. E.L. Magoon, *Orators of the American Revolution* (New York, 1857), reprinted by Sightext Publications, El Segundo, CA, 1969, p. 208.
6. John Eidsmoe, *Christianity and the Constitution* (Grand Rapids, 1987), p. 376.
7. CHOC, p. IV-V.
8. Foster and Swanson, p. 37.
9. Foster and Swanson, pp. 106-107.

Chapter 10

1. Newton Hall and Irving Wood, *Book of Life* (Chicago, 1956).
2. *Book of Life,* Vol. 8, pp. 98-105.
3. J. Lee Grady, "Journalism and the Gospel," *Providential Perspective*, Vol.6 No. 7 (Charlottesville, Va., 1991).
4. Ted Baehr, *The Christian Family Guide to Movies and Video, Vol. 2* (Nashville, 199).
5. Franky Schaeffer, *A Time for Anger (Westchester, IL, 1982), p. 149.*
6. Grady, "Journalism and the Gospel."

Chapter 11

1. Montesquieu, *The Spirit of Laws*, quoted in CHOC, pp. 134-135.

Chapter 12

1. Charles Hull Wolfe, "The Principle Approach to American Christian Economics," in *A Guide to American Christian Education for the Home and School, the Principle Approach* (Palo Cedro, CA, 1990). All the quotes in this chapter not footnoted are from this article by Wolfe.
2. Greg Anthony, *Biblical Economics* (Charlottesville, 1988), p. 13.
3. *How to Understand the Purpose behind Humanism,* Institute in Basic Youth Conflicts, 1983, p. 7.
4. William Bradford, *Of Plimoth Plantation*, pp. 162-163.
5. John Locke, *Of Civil Government,* quoted in CHOC, p. 64.
6. Slater, p. 234.
7. Slater, pp. 228-229.

8. George Grant, *In the Shadow of Plenty* (Fort Worth, 1986), p. 4.
9. Rosalie J. Slater, "Noah Webster, Founding Father of American Scholarship and Education," an article that prefaces the facsimile reprint of *Webster's 1828 Dictionary*, p. 14.
10. Gary DeMar, *God and Government, Vol. 2, Issues in Biblical Perspective* (Atlanta, 1984), pp. 131, 121.
11. Anthony, p. 34.
12. Chilton, quoted in Anthony, p. 34.
13. Anthony, p. 34.
14. David Chilton, *Productive Christians in an Age of Guilt Manipulators: A Biblical Response to Ronald J. Sider*, quoted in Anthony, p. 27.
15. Anthony, p. 28.
16. Anthony, pp. 28-29.

Chapter 13

1. Eidsmoe, p. 364.
2. *Our Ageless Constitution*, edited by W. David Stedman and LaVaughn G. Lewis (Asheboro, NC, 1987), p. 39.
3. Ibid.
4. Gary North, *Healer of the Nations, Biblical Principles for International Relations* (Fort Worth, 1987), p. 11.
5. North.
6. North.
7. Lee Grady, "Can We Make a Deal for Peace?" The Forerunner, Vol. VIII, No. 8, Deceember 1987, pp. 15-17.

Bibliography

Alexander, David, and Pat Alexander, editors. *Eerdmans' Handbook to the Bible*. Grand Rapids: William B. Eerdmans Publishing Co., 1973.

Amos, Gary T. *Defending the Declaration*. Brentwood, Tennessee: Wolgemuth & Hyatt, 1989.

Anthony, Greg. *Biblical Economics*. Charlottesville, Virginia: Providence Foundation, 1988.

Baldwin, Alice. *The New England Clergy and the American Revolution*. Fredick Ungar Pub. Co., 1928.

Bancroft, George. *History of the United States of America*. 10 volumes. D. Appleton and Co., 1891.

Barret, David. *Cosmos, Chaos, and Gospel, a Chronology of World Evangelization from Creation to New Creation*. Birmingham, AL: New Hope, 1987.

Barton, David. *Myth of Separation*. Aledo, Texas: Wallbuilder Press, 1989.

Beliles, Mark A., and McDowell, Stephen K. *America's Providential History*. Charlottesville: Providence Foundation, 1989.

Blumenfeld, Samuel L. *Is Public Education Necessary?* Boise, Idaho: The Paradigm Company, 1985.

Blumenfeld, Samuel L. *NEA: Trojan Horse in American Education*, Boise, Idaho: The Paradigm Company, 1985.

Bradford, William. *Of Plimoth Plantation*. Boston: Wright & Potter Printing Co., 1901.

Brutus, Junius. *A Defense of Liberty Against Tyrants (Vindiciae Contra Tyrannos)*. Edmonton, AB Canada: Still Waters Revival Books, reprinted from the 1689 translation, 1989.

Calvin, John. *Institutes of the Christian Religion*. Philadelphia. Presbyterian Board of Publication.

Chilton, David. *Productive Christians in an Age of Guilt Manipulators: A*

Biblical Response to Ronald J. Sider. Tyler, TX: Institute for Christian Economics, 1982.

Chilton, David. "Alfred the Great," *Equity,* the newsletter of the Christian Public Policy Council, January, 1989.

Christopher Columbus's Book of Prophecies, Reproduction of the Original Manuscript with English Translation by Kay Brigham. Quincentenary Edition. Barcelona, Spain: CLIE Publishers.

Coffin, Charles Carleton. *The Story of Liberty.* New York: Harper & Brothers, 1878.

Cord, Robert L. *Separation of Church and State.* New York: Lambeth Press, 1982.

D'Aubigne, J.H. Merle. *History of the Reformation of the Sixteenth Century.* Translated by H. White. New York: Hurst & Company.

Demar, Gary. *God and Government, Vol. 1, A Biblical and Historical Study.* Atlanta: American Vision Press, 1982.

Demar, Gary. *God and Government, Vol. 2, Issues in Biblical Perspective.* Atlanta: American Vision Press, 1984.

DeMar, Gary. *"You've Heard It Said."* Brentwood, TN: Wolgemuth & Hyatt, 1991.

Dorchester, Daniel. *Christianity in the United States.* New York: Hunt & Eaton, 1895.

Dreisbach, Daniel L. *Real Threat and Mere Shadow, Religious Liberty and the First Amendment.* Westchester, Illinois: Crossway Books, 1987.

Edwards, Brian. *God's Outlaw.* Wheaton, Illinois: Tyndale House Publishers, Inc., 1981.

Eidsmoe, John. *Christianity and the Constitution.* Grand Rapids, Michigan: Baker Book House, 1987.

Eidsmoe, John. *God & Caesar, Christian Faith & Political Action.* Westchester, IL: Crossway Books, 1987.

Finney, Charles G. *Revivals of Religion.* Virginia Beach, VA: CBN University Press, 1978.

Fiske, John. *The Beginnings of New England.* New York: Houghton, Mifflin and Co., 1898.

Foster, Marshall, and Mary-Elaine Swanson. *The American Covenant the Untold Story.* California: Mayflower Institute, 1983.

Frothingham, Richard. *The Rise of the Republic of the United States.* Boston: Little, Brown, and Co., 1895.

Gaustad, Edwin Scott. *A Religious History of America.* New York: Harper & Row, 1974.

Grady, J. Lee. "Journalism and the Gospel," *Providential Perspective,* Vol.6 No.7, Charlottesville, VA: Providence Foundation, 1991.

Grady, J. Lee. "Can We Make a Deal for Peace?" *The Forerunner,* Vol. VIII, No. 8, December 1987.

Grant, George. *In the Shadow of Plenty.* Fort Worth, Texas: Dominion Press, 1986.

Guyot, Arnold. *The Earth and Man.* Boston: Gould and Lincoln, 1863.

Guyot, Arnold. *Physical Geography.* New York: Ivison, Blakeman and Co., 1885.

Hakluyt, Richard (1552-1616). *A Selection of the Principal Voyages, Traffiques and Discoveries of the English Nation.* With a Preface by Laurence Irving. New York: Alfred A. Knopf, 1926.

Halbrook, Stephen P. *That Every Man Be Armed, the Evolution of a Constitutional Right.* Oakland, CA: The Independent Institute, 1984.

Hall, Newton Marshall, and Wood, Irving Francis, editors. *The Book of Life,* in 8 volumes. Chicago: John Rudin & Company, 1956.

Hall, Verna M., and Rosalie J. Slater. *The Bible and the Constitution of the United States of America.* San Francisco: Foundation for American Christian Education, 1983.

Hall, Verna M., compiler. *The Christian History of the American Revolution, Consider and Ponder.* San Francisco: Foundation for American Christian Education, 1976.

Hall, Verna M., compiler. *The Christian History of the Constitution of the United States of America, Christian Self-Government.* San Francisco: Foundation for American Christian Education, 1980.

Hall, Verna M., compiler. *The Christian History of the Constitution of the United States of America, Christian Self-Government with Union.* San Francisco: Foundation for American Christian Education, 1979.

Hamilton, Alexander, James Madison and John Jay. *The Federalist Papers.* First published in 1787-1788. New York: Bantam Books, 1988.

Hardinge, Leslie. *The Celtic Church in Britain.* London: Church Historical

Society, 1973.

"How to Understand the Purpose Behind Humanism." Institute in Basic Youth Conflicts, 1983.

Johnson, William J. *George Washington the Christian.* Reprinted by Mott Media, Milford, MI., 1976.

Lutz, Donald S. "The Relative Influence of European Writers on Late Eighteenth-Century American Political Thought," *American Political Science Review,* Vol. 78, 1984.

Madison, James. *Notes of Debates in the Federal Convention of 1787 Reported by James Madison.* New York: W.W. Norton & Co., 1987.

Magoon, E.L. *Orators of the American Revolution.* New York: C. Scribner, 1857. Reprinted by Sightext Publications, El Segundo, California, 1969.

Marshall, Peter, and David Manuel. *The Light and the Glory.* Old Tappan, New Jersey: Fleming H. Revell, 1977.

Marshall, Peter, and David Manuel. *From Sea to Shining Sea.* Old Tappan, New Jersey: Fleming H. Revell, 1986.

McLaughlin, Andrew C. *Foundations of American Constitutionalism.* Greenwich, Conn.: Fawcett Publications, Inc., 1966.

Montesquieu, Baron De. *The Spirit of Laws.* Translated by Thomas Nugent. New York: the Colonial Press, 1899.

Morris, B.F. *Christian Life and Character of the Civil Institutions of the United States.* Philadelphia: George W. Childs, 1864.

Motley, John Lothrop. *The Rise of the Dutch Republic.* 3 Volumes. New York: Harper & Brothers, 1855.

Neander, Dr. Augustus. *General History of the Christian Religion and Church.* Translated from the German by Joseph Torrey. London: Henry G. Bohn, 1851.

North, Gary. *Healer of the Nations, Biblical Principles for International Relations.* Fort Worth, Texas: Dominion Press, 1987.

North, Gary. *Honest Money,* Biblical Principles of Money and Banking. Ft. Worth, Texas: Dominion Press, 1986.

Norval, Morgan, editor. *The Militia in 20th Century America: a Symposium.* Falls Church, VA: Gun Owners Foundation, 1985.

Old South Leaflets. Published by The Old South Association, Old South Meeting-house, Boston, Mass.

Peck, Jesse T. *The History of the Great Republic, Considered from a Christian Standpoint.* New York: Broughton and Wyman, 1868.

Pope, Norman V. "Educator, Minister, Patriot," in *Nation Under God,* Frances Brentano, editor. Great Neck, New York: Channel Press, 1957.

Powell, Edward A., and Rousas John Rushdoony. *Tithing and Dominion.* Vallecito, CA: Ross House Books, 1982.

Remember William Penn, 1644-1944, a Tercentenary Memorial. Compiled by the William Penn Tercentenary Committee. Harrisburg, PA: Commonwealth of Pennsylvania, 1945.

Rollin, Charles. *The Ancient History of the Egyptians, Carthaginians, Assyrians, Babylonians, Medes and Persians, Grecians, and Macedonians; including a History of the Arts and Sciences of the Ancients.* 2 volumes. New York: George Dearborn, 1836.

Rose, James B. *A Guide to American Christian Education for the Home and School, the Principle Approach.* Palo Cedro, CA: American Christian History Institute.

Rushdoony, Rousas John. *The Institutes of Biblical Law.* The Presbyterian and Reformed Publishing Company, 1973.

Rutherford, Samuel. *Lex Rex, or The Law and the Prince.* First published in 1644. Reprint, Harrisonburg, Va: Sprinkle Publications, 1982.

Sandoz, Ellis, editor. *Political Sermons of the American Founding Era, 1730-1805.* Indianapolis: Liberty Press, 1991.

Schaeffer, Francis A. *How Should We Then Live?* Old Tappan, New Jersey: Fleming H. Revell Company, 1976.

Schaeffer, Francis A. *A Christian Manifesto.* Westchester, Illinois: Crossway Books, 1982.

Sidney, Algernon. *Discourses Concerning Government.* Edited by Thomas G. West. Indianapolis: Liberty Classics, 1990.

Skousen, W. Cleon. *The Making of America.* Washington, D.C.: The National Center for Constitutional Studies, 1985.

Slater, Rosalie J. *Teaching and Learning America's Christian History, the Principle Approach.* San Francisco: Foundation for American Christian Education, 1980.

Slater, Rosalie J. An essay on Noah Webster in the preface to a reprint of *An American Dictionary of the English Language* by Noah Webster, 1828. San

Francisco: Foundation for American Christian Education, 1980.

Stedman, W. David, and LaVaughn G. Lewis, editors. *Our Ageless Constitution*. Asheboro, NC: W. David Stedman Associates, 1987.

Stoel, Caroline P., and Ann B. Clarke. *Magna Carta, Liberty Under the Law*. Portland, Oregon: published jointly by Magna Carta in America and Graphic Arts Center Publishing Co., 1986.

Thornton, John Wingate. *The Pulpit of the American Revolution*. Boston: Gould & Lincoln, 1860.

Tocqueville, Alexis de. *Democracy in America*. Edited by J.P. Mayer. Garden City, NY: Doubleday & Co., Inc., 1969.

Walton, Rus. *One Nation Under God*. Nashville: Thomas Nelson, 1987.

Walton, Rus. *Biblical Solutions to Contemporary Problems*. Brentwood, Tennessee: Wolgemuth & Hyatt, 1988.

Webster, Noah. *History of the United States*. New Haven: Durrie & Peck, 1833.

Wells, William V. *The Life and Public Services of Samuel Adams*. 3 volumes. Boston: Little, Brown, and Company, 1865.

Whitehead, John W. *The Second American Revolution*. Elgin, Illinois: David C. Cook Publishing Co., 1982.

Willard, Emma. *A System of Universal History in Perspective*. Hartford: F.J. Huntington, 1835.

The Providence Foundation

The purpose of the Providence Foundation is to assist in spreading liberty, justice, and prosperity among the nations by teaching and equipping people in a biblical philosophy of life. Emphasis is upon educating in principles, rather than issues, drawing upon examples in history for illustration. The founding era of America's history is especially emphasized since ideas of Divine Providence and similar terminology expressed a basic link in the Founders' thinking between God and history.

"Providence" is defined as the preservation, government, guidance and direction which God exercises over all creation including the civil affairs of men and women. The Scriptures contain a theology of the family, the church, and the state. Principles in God's written Word that relate to civil government, politics, economics, and education are timeless and universally useful for the benefit of any culture on earth today.

We seek to accomplish our purpose through the following objectives: 1. Teach people in general in Christian principles of law, government and politics, economics and business, arts and sciences, education and family life through seminars, presentations, and consultation. 2. Equip and train leaders and Foundation representatives who will train others via teaching classes, leading study groups, establishing action groups, etc. 3. Provide books, tapes, videos, and other resources.

We seek to serve those who have a desire to help others: parents and teachers and scholars; pastors and church leaders; public officials and social activists.

Our long term goal is to restore to America's homes, churches, and schools the ideas that form the foundation of freedom as well as to infuse these same ideas into the fabric of all nations. The training we provide is with the goal of having individuals apply the principles they learn, the result being godly reform in all spheres of life.

About the Authors

Stephen McDowell , Executive Director of the Providence Foundation, has taught inspiring seminars throughout the United States as well as in Asia, South America, Australia, and Africa. He has trained thousands of people from 70 countries, consulted with numerous government officials, assisted in writing political documents and starting political parties, and helped establish classes on godly reformation in numerous churches. He has authored and co-authored several books and videos. After obtaining a B.S. in Physics and a M.S. in Geology, Stephen went on to work in the ministry. He pastored churches for six years before moving to Charlottesville to help Mark Beliles start the Providence Foundation. He and his wife, Beth, have four children.

Mark Beliles has served in the ministry since 1977 and is presently the pastor of Grace Covenant Church in Charlottesville, Virginia. His concern for equipping pastors and Christians in applying biblical principles to all of life led him to help start the Providence Foundation in 1983, from which time he has served as President. He has authored and co-authored several books, has participated in training many Christian leaders for the ministry, has taught seminars on biblical reformation throughout the United States and in other countries, and has assisted in establishing churches in America and other nations. Mark and his wife, Nancy, have three children.

Resource Order Form

Order from: **Providence Foundation**, P.O. Box 6759, Charlottesville, VA 22906

	Price	Qty.	Total

BOOKS

America's Providential History — $14.95 ____ ____

How the Lord guided our nation from the very beginning. Proof from history: our nation grew from Christian principles. How to bring them back into the mainstream.

Liberating the Nations — $11.95 ____ ____

God's plan, fundamental principles, essential foundations, and structures necessary to build Christian nations.

Defending the Declaration — $10.95 ____ ____

How the Bible and Christianity influenced the writing of the Declaration of Independence.

In God We Trust — $6.95 ____ ____

A Christian tour guide for historic sites in Washington D.C., Philadelphia and parts of Virginia.

Watchmen on the Walls — $5.95 ____ ____

The role of pastors in equipping Christians to fulfill their civil duties.

Jefferson's Abridgement — $5.95 ____ ____

An abridgement of the Words of Jesus of Nazareth as compiled by Thomas Jefferson while President. With an introductory essay on Jefferson's religious beliefs.

In Search of Democracy — $4.95 ____ ____

The foundations, framework, and historical development of biblical government and law.

Videos/Game

The Story of America's Liberty — $19.95 ____ ____

A 60 minute look at the influence of Christianity in the beginning of America, examining principles and providential occurrences.

Dawn's Early Light — $19.95 ____ ____

A 28 minute version of The Story of America's Liberty.

America: the Game — $29.95 ____ ____

An exciting way to learn about the history of America and God's hand in it.

Audios

The Greatest Story Never Told: The Story of America's Liberty	$4.95	____ ____

Christianity was the foundation of America's character and institutions and is the source of our freedom, prosperity, and greatness.

"No Cross, No Crown"	$4.95	____ ____

Exemplified in the Life of William Penn

Reforming the Nations	$4.95	____ ____

An example from the life of Noah Webster

Teaching History from a Providential Perspective	$4.95	____ ____
The Principle Approach	$4.95	____ ____

A Christian philosophy and methodology of education.

God Governs in the Affairs of Men	$4.95	____ ____
Biblical Economics	$4.95	____ ____
Honest Money and Banking	$4.95	____ ____
Biblical Government and Law	$4.95	____ ____
Forming a Christian Union	$4.95	____ ____
Fundamental Principles of Christian Nations	$4.95	____ ____
Christ's Teaching on Public Affairs	$4.95	____ ____
The Principle Approach to Education for Home or Church Schools	$99.95	____ ____

A biblical approach to teaching the academic subjects. Includes 24 tapes and a 160-page manual.

In Search of Democracy	$14.95	____ ____

Four tape series that accompanies book.

Subtotal		____
Shipping (10% with $2.50 minimum; Game $4.50)		____
TOTAL:		____

Name:_____ Phone:_____

Address:_____

City_____ State_____ Zip_____